Guilt, Se

An Unrehearsed Life

Joan Lynn Faust

Front cover design by Tamzin C. Tilley.

Layout and formatting by Remi Bronson.

First printing edition 2018. ISBN 978-0-692-15172-3.

First digital edition 2018. AISN B07FC62NF9.

Works used with permission:

This book is dedicated to the memory of

Grace and Isabelle

Table of Contents

Acknowledgements

If it weren't for my grandson, Remi, asking me to help him with an assignment for school in 1998 at age 12, I may never have written this book. He needed to interview someone who lived during WWII. While writing the essay, I remembered being praised for a short story I wrote in high school about a neighbor's housekeeper helping me cut school by pretending to be my mother on the phone with the school nurse. That thought encouraged me to start a memoir about Aunt Grace.

In 2000, I enrolled in a writing class at the New School in New York. At the time I was happily involved with acting classes and auditioning. Those pursuits took precedence over writing classes. However, I continued working on the Grace story.

In 2004, my dear friend, Laura Middleton, told me that she had taken a class at the Gotham Writers Workshop and thought it was excellent. "You should sign up as soon as possible for the memoir class," she said softly with a smile, "It will help your writing considerably."

"Thanks!" I said.

"I didn't mean it that way," she said, in all innocence. But of course she did. It was part of her charm.

Laura and I read each other's work and gave each other feedback through the years. In order to finance her travel habit, she held down two jobs, which eventually forced her to take on proposal writing for extra money, leaving pleasure writing for a future time, a time that never came. However, she encouraged me to keep at it, and was a major participant in editing my work.

In 2017, while fighting cancer, Laura wanted to learn self-publishing and offered to use my work for a trial run. During a period of remission, she moved to California and continued treatment there. When she informed me that she called in hospice, I travelled to be by her side for several days. She told me one thing she regretted was not being able to keep her promise. I lay beside her, held her tightly, told her how much I loved her, and cried. She passed away shortly after. This acknowledgement is not only for her encouragement and support, but for her friendship, her loyalty, her uplifting spirit, and for the joy she brought to my life.

Prior to any thought of publishing, I'd like to thank family members who gave me valuable suggestions through the years–Remi, my daughter Jenny, my sister Peppi.

I must thank Matt Swope, personal trainer for my husband and me, who edited my day's writings while I walked on the treadmill.

Gretl Clagget and Shelly Stenhouse, writing teachers at the 92Y, were among the formidable teachers who gave me on-the-mark critiques. Fellow student Phyllis Brusiloff went through my work like a paid editor, and Dorothy Furman was happy to read and comment on my work whenever asked. Special gratitude goes to these two friends.

Theresa Burns, my book editor and current teacher at the 92Y, has been instrumental in helping me cultivate a writing style through the past five years. Her suggestions were positive and precise. The painstaking effort Theresa put into correcting my manuscript's punctuation mistakes alone deserves my highest praise and deepest gratitude.

Now I was on my own to self-publish. The mere thought of it overwhelmed me. I contacted lulu.com and chose the option to pay them to do the work. But they were fearful about being sued over trivial, misunderstood details in the manuscript, and wanted me to make unnecessary changes, which included using a penname. After much thought, I backed out of the deal, did the work I could, and called upon my family to give me help with the rest.

This book would not have been published without their help.

My grandson, Remi, took on the burden of guiding me through the process of getting my book in shape for publishing, including making decisions on adding and rewriting passages that my editor suggested I make, and reading the sample book for errors; a daunting task, for sure.

My granddaughter, Tamzin, designer of the book cover, put her personal work aside to spend hours with me designing flyers and e-mails to help publicize the book. Because of her cheery, loving disposition, she kept calm as I made changes with every sample printing until we reached perfection.

Jenny, insisted there be an *About the Author* segment on the back cover, and took it upon herself to write one, for which I am most grateful. I can confirm that every word of it is true.

I cannot thank these loved ones enough for their time, encouragement and love.

Grace

"Joan Gruber, report to the office. You have a phone call." The words blared from our second-rate public address system. It was the summer of 1950; I was eleven. As far back as I can remember, my parents shipped me off to one camp or another every June for eight weeks. No argument could exempt me from being sent away.

Mother was sitting at her vanity table preparing for a charity luncheon the day I entered her bedroom and voiced my protest. "I don't want to go to camp. Everybody there hates me!"

"I'm sure not everyone hates you dear. How could they dislike a sweet girl like you?" She leaned into the mirror and plucked at her eyebrows.

"Well they do!" I belly flopped onto her four-poster antique bed and rolled until I faced her. "And besides, I get teased all the time."

"What do they tease you about, Joanie?" I let my hands dangle down from the bed and played with the soft cotton bed skirt. Mother went to her walk-in closet to pick a dress. As president of the local chapter of Hadassah, she had to chair the meeting and make a speech.

"Everything! They make fun of my stringy straight hair. They make fun of my last name by calling me Goober or Grubber and say I'm too gawky to play on their team." I jumped from the bed and followed her into the closet. "Oh Mommy," I cried, grabbing her around the waist, "Please let me stay home. I promise, promise, promise I won't get in your way!"

Holding a hanger high in her right hand, she patted me on the head with her left. "They're jealous of you, honey. Just laugh them off. Show them you're a good sport." I lowered my head. She lifted my chin toward hers, looked into my eyes with assurance and said, "I promise the teasing will stop." I believed her advice should be taken, although I doubted I could carry it out.

Mother pulled another hanger from the rod. "Which dress do you think I should wear?" I pointed to the vibrant floral dress with a full skirt and scooped neckline. The other dress was an embroidered white sundress with a straight skirt, spaghetti straps, and matching bolero jacket. It was beautiful, but I preferred color. She placed the flowered dress back on the rod, and continued, "Besides, you'll be bored staying home. All your friends are away for the summer. What will you do? Sleep all day?"

My parents, Jack and Isabelle, had a very active social life at the Preakness Hills Country Club during the summer. They golfed all morning, played cards in the afternoon, and danced at night. I knew that was why they sent me to camp. While my father enjoyed showing off Isabelle, who was beautiful and a clothes horse, my mother reveled in showing off the seasons' fashions from Bonwit Teller, and her Tiffany jewelry.

"Camp builds character," she continued as she stepped into her dress. "You'll learn how to get along with others and you won't get teased anymore. The good news is you'll have your sister with you. Won't that be nice?" Of course it wasn't nice. Peppi was three years older than me and no angel.

One stormy winter night when our parents were out, I was frightened to be alone in my room. I grabbed my pillow and knocked on Peppi's door. Her room was bigger than mine, with a row of windows that faced the street. I loved to look out and gaze at the slender, twisted tree trunk and green leaves that spread across the bottom of the windows. On rainy days, I'd sneak into her room, watch cars whiz by, and listen to the sound of tires on wet road.

"What do you want, *brat?*" Peppi shouted from her antique four-poster bed. It seemed everyone in the family had an antique four-poster bed except me.

"I'm scared, can I stay with you?" I cried, clutching the pillow tight against my chest.

"Well, you're not helpless. Open the door and come in." I climbed onto the bed and snuggled up next to her. "P.U. You stink, Yuck Face," she squealed. "Move your carcass to the foot of the bed and sleep by my *sweet smelling* feet." She pointed to the exact spot where she wanted me. I curled up like a dog and did not move until our parents came home and carried me back to my room.

One Saturday morning I walked into Peppi's room while she was brushing her hair in front of the full length mirror on her closet door. She was in a dress, which was unusual. She preferred wearing slacks or a skirt and sweater. "Where are you going?" I asked.

"Why?" she responded.

"I just want to know." I walked over to the window to look at the tree and down to the top of the striped awning that shaded the front porch.

"Y?" she parroted, glancing at herself in the mirror.

"I'm just curious!" I peered into her walk-in closet. It seemed everyone had a walk-in closet but me.

"Y?"

This "why" question and answer nonsense continued as Peppi walked downstairs and into the kitchen with me trailing behind. Mother was having coffee, and I immediately complained about Peppi not telling me where she was going. Mother gave Peppi a quizzical look, as if to ask, "*Why* won't you tell her?"

"I told her," Peppi insisted.

"SHE DID NOT!"

"I told her I was going to the *Y*." I didn't think that was funny. I thought it was mean.

I never felt like an important part of the family. It was a household of three, and I was an afterthought. I was like a tattered flag buffeted by constant winds propelling me in different directions. I simply acted in accord with the strongest gust.

As a very young child, I was never sure if I was to be included in family activities. If I heard plans being made, I'd ask "Me, too?" It wasn't long before "Yes, you are" turned into "Oh look, it's *Me*

Too Gruber." What did it matter? At the time, being included was comfort enough for me. I reacted to Mother's praise, Peppi's tease, and Father's discipline with a sense of belonging.

When Peppi and I were little, we would run to the door when Father came home and sit on one of his shoes as he walked around asking, "Why do my legs feel so heavy?" We giggled with glee. He could wiggle his ears and did so at our command. At dinner, his job was to step on the buzzer underneath the carpet to call for Lena, who was our housekeeper for as long as I can remember. He never found it on the first try and moved his foot around incessantly before Lena pushed the swinging door open. "Did you buzz?" she asked, grinning. We never knew if it was the buzzer or our laughter that brought her through the door.

As we grew older, Father became less playful, more critical, and frequently gruff. When I was six, Mother gave me some outdated costume jewelry, a few old party gowns, and a pair of shoes that hurt her feet. When Father walked into the den and saw me dressed to the nines in Mother's clothes, he asked, "What are you doing?"

"Playing Princess," I said.

Born in 1939 at the outbreak of World War II, I was raised on stories about the heroic efforts of Princess Elizabeth, who, to quote the news, supported her *parents' efforts to keep up the morale of the English people.* The princess was praised continually on all the radio stations. Every young girl wanted to be like Elizabeth, and I was no exception.

In a critical tone Father replied, "Joan, do you know how hard it is to be a princess? You always have to get good marks, obey your parents, and keep yourself groomed and looking perfectly coiffed. You can't pick your own friends, but are subject to the rigors of royalty. You must always be well-informed, alert to your surroundings, and courteous to everyone you meet."

I was devastated. That was too much information for one little girl to handle. Maybe he meant well, but that incident stifled my imaginary thoughts, and fantasy play became a private matter kept well within the confines of my room, open only to my closest friends.

When I was in seventh grade, I mentioned to Father that I had a yen for chocolate chip cookies. He reprimanded, "There's no such word as yen. Where do you pick up such words?" I was speechless and believed I had gotten the word wrong. Mother's constant instructions to always look nice and behave well when he was around heightened my perception of him as a disciplinarian.

Our evening meal around the antique dining room table was the only time the four of us ever sat together. Father's presence in the house was limited. He arrived home from work at six and spent most weekends at the club. Mother spent her days playing mahjong, canasta, or bridge, or volunteering at one of the many charities she supported. Occasionally, she found time to share gossip, instruct me on how to act in public, or coach me on how to dress. But finding time to help me with homework or school projects was out of the question.

Dinner began promptly at 6:30. I always sat quietly, using my best table manners and waiting to be praised for my good behavior, while my sister constantly brought up controversial subjects, luring my father into a debate. Whatever Father's opinion, Peppi chose the opposing view. Even though I had no understanding of any of the topics, I sided with her, hoping this would bring positive support from my nemesis. When Peppi learned about labor unions and the Taft-Hartley Act, she asked if Father's plant was unionized. "Certainly not," Father exclaimed, and the battle was on. Peppi supported the workers' right to organize for better conditions and higher pay from tyrannical bosses. Father said he paid his employees very well, the factory conditions were just fine, and workers got a fifteen minute morning coffee break that always rolled into twenty. He complained that the unions insisted they get a second time-out. He ended the discussion with, "What the hell they need two coffee breaks for in one morning, I'll never know."

When Father was twelve, he ran away from home in 1915 to stay with relatives in Princeton, N.J. He earned money by selling newspapers to the students at the university. His mother had died less than a year before, and his father remarried the first woman presented to him by the family, who turned out to be the proverbial wicked stepmother. She had five children of her own and used my father and his two sisters as Cinderellas.

It was decades before I understood why Father was so pragmatic. Time with him was spent in silence or I withdrew from him altogether. Through the years, I slowly came to appreciate this self-made man and was able to forgive him for squelching my imagination and inhibiting my creativity.

One of the wealthy students at Princeton saw potential in my father and paid for agricultural studies for him on a nearby farm, where he learned the difference between the Holstein and Jersey cows which grazed on the farmland grass. But Father had a different calling and quit. He found work as a salesman with the Melina Company selling textiles, learned all about the industry, and finally established *Facil Fabrics* in Paterson, N.J., a company that manufactured decorative materials. He invented a system of lamination to bond silky threads onto a smooth backing to produce beautiful ribbons, bows, and packaging. The self-stick bows are very popular around the holiday season and can still be purchased at any stationery store. These brightly colored, perfectly shaped bows, give a professional look to any gift box. He partnered with friends to buy industrial and commercial real estate during a time when Paterson was booming with industry. He was generous, kind, and known in the community as a good and honest businessman. He never held a grudge and financially supported his father and step-mother in their later years as well as his step-brothers and sisters.

My mother also came from humble beginnings and often used the cliché, "I've been rich and I've been poor, and you know what? I like rich better." She promised my father to continue working after they married, but soon after, she quit her job as a buyer for McCrory's, a five-and-ten-cent store that went out of business in 1938, a year before I was born.

I loved hearing stories about my parents' courtship, like the time Mother accidently made two dates for the same night, one with my father and one with Saint Clair Campbell Makai. When they both showed up, she told my father that he had the day wrong. "Our date is for tomorrow night," she said. Not surprisingly, he left and never showed up the following evening. Sometime later, they bumped into each other on the subway. Mother apologized for the mix up and told him she would very much like to reschedule a date. He said, "How about tonight?"

She replied, "I actually have a date tonight, but just to show you how much I'd like to make it up to you, I'm going to cancel the other date and you can pick me up at 7:00." She didn't have another date. My father showed up and the romance began.

Isabelle liked making dinner dates with Jack. During their courtship, she was living at home with her two brothers and her sick mother. Money was scarce, and dinner dates helped cut down on expenses. No matter where they went for dinner, mother made sure they sat near the window. Her two brothers would *mysteriously* walk by, and she would wave them in to their table. Jack had no alternative but to feed them. Every so often he would give them each a quarter for a movie so he could be alone with Isabelle.

After the relationship was in full swing, Jack invited Isabelle for dinner and dancing at his country club in Bedford, NY. "Wear your prettiest dress," he suggested. Mother bought an outfit for the occasion, adorned herself with her best costume jewelry, and spent an hour in front of the mirror making sure she looked perfect. She was not only a hit with my father, she was the belle of the ball.

Mother saw lobster as a choice on the menu and decided it was a good chance to taste it for the first time. "Is it good?" she asked Jack.

"Delicious," he said.

"I'd like to try it," she said.

Jack smiled, and wisely abandoned his idea of ordering one for himself. He chose the porterhouse steak, discreetly asking Isabelle how she liked a steak cooked. As he suspected, after Isabelle took one bite of lobster, the plates were switched.

He invited Mother to the club a second time for a swim. He rode up early in the morning with his buddies for a round of golf, leaving his car for her to drive up at leisure. "I'll meet you at the pool when I'm finished playing," he said. She asked if it was alright for her sister, Gracie, and brother-in-law, Don, to join them. He had no objection.

Gracie was apprehensive about leaving her dog alone for that long a time. Mother thought it wouldn't be a problem for a tiny Maltese to come along, always wanting Gracie to feel happy and peaceful, as she suffered from anxiety and depression.

They pulled up to valet parking, and Gracie emerged with fluffy white Fifi in her arms. "Dogs are not allowed in a country club, Ma'am," the attendant said.

Gracie grumbled. "Isabelle, you said there wouldn't be a problem."

"It's such a little dog," Isabelle pleaded. "Can't you make an exception just this once?"

They couldn't. The dog spent the day in the car with each of them taking turns giving him water and a walk around the parking lot. The dog made it perfectly clear that he was not happy about the arrangement by chewing the car upholstery to shreds.

Considering Father's first-date mishap, having to feed Mother's brothers, foregoing a lobster dinner, and having his car ruined, I often wonder what possessed him to marry her.

The summer of 1950 was half over by the time my name was announced over the loud speakers that day at camp. I was suffering through tennis lessons, trying desperately to get the ball over the net. My heart danced with excitement as I thought about what the call could mean: first, that my mother was thinking about me, and second, that the announcement had reached the ears of every camper and counselor. This made me feel quite special.

It was a brutally hot afternoon in July, so I happily left the court to cool off beneath the canopy of trees lining the path to the camp office.

The 36 acres of Camp Woodlands were set in Maine's Lakes Region and were surrounded by mountains. It was the most beautiful and secluded of the camps where I summered. I enjoyed walking down the many flowering lanes. My favorite pathway led to a grassy field where I loved to hide in the long green blades of grass under an old oak tree. I'd select the perfect spot about four feet from the trunk where the overhead leaves sprinkled the ground with circles of sunlight and patches of shade. I'd lie on my back and watch the clouds rearrange themselves into different shapes and sizes: large ones like whales or monsters and small ones like a string of pearls or a row of marching mice. My favorites looked like furry, four-legged animals. I pretended they were alive and made up stories about them, like the lion and the lioness moving closer and closer together, changing form until they blended into one because they couldn't bear to live apart. I was convinced love was like that, although I doubted I would ever find a boy to want me that much.

I was so excited as I hurried to the office that I didn't notice passing my favorite pathway. Approaching the open field, where we assembled every morning for flag raising, I ran as fast as I could to avoid the blazing sun.

When I reached the office, I was given an unusually warm and friendly greeting. "Take the call in here," said Miss Anne, the owner of the camp, a middle-aged woman with clownish red hair and a cheerless disposition, "it will be more private." She led me toward the inner office where campers were not usually welcomed, and motioned me toward the desk phone.

Why is she being so nice to me? She's always so mean, shouting commands and giving everyone dirty looks. It was the first time I ever saw a smile on her face. I'd never seen her treat anyone so tenderly. Miss Anne closed the door softly and left the room. I felt so grown-up as I walked over to the desk and picked up the phone. "Hello," I said, as though I were asking a question. It was Mother.

"Hi sweetheart, how are you?"

"I'm fine," I said hesitantly. Something in her voice made me aware of my beating heart, and I sank into Miss Anne's swivel chair beside the phone.

"I have some bad news," she said, in a hushed tone. I became rigid, held my breath, and waited.

"Aunt Grace is in the hospital. She has pneumonia and is really sick. I thought I should tell you because she may not make it through the night."

I pressed the receiver to my ear, swiveling fiercely and staring at the ceiling to keep back my tears. "Don't say that," I finally said, "she won't die. She has to make it! I love her too much. I'll pray to God, Mommy. You pray, too, and she won't die. I just know she won't die."

*****

Aunt Grace was my mother's younger sister and my savior. She kept me from feeling alone and unwanted. Her home was located between my school and my house, permitting frequent visits. She treated me like her own daughter, asking me to help her make beds, stir sauces, or wash dishes. I'd play with Jimmy, her younger child, and she trusted me to take him to the railroad station to watch trains come and go. Holding Jimmy's hand and teaching him how to cross busy 20th Avenue made me feel needed and grown up. I also adored Jimmy's older brother, Harmon, who was in high school. When he brought his friends home after school, I worshiped them the same way I idolized Frank Sinatra and Cary Grant.

Sometimes Aunt Grace sat me at her vanity table, brushed my hair and pinned it up and put lipstick and rouge on my face. She dressed me in her party dresses, giving free expression to the creativity repressed by Father's insensitive remark when I was playing Princess at age six.

I wanted to be just like Gracie: warmhearted, generous, married to a man who kissed me hello and goodbye, and a career man who commuted by train. I also hoped I would be a mother who was admired and loved by her children.

Gracie and my mother looked very much alike – both beautiful and stylish. They could compete with Elizabeth Taylor in a beauty contest, and the judge would be hard pressed to select a winner.

A photograph of my mother and Gracie facing each other in profile sat on a table in our living room. Each had wavy, golden brown hair in an upsweep with the curls billowing out into a crown of loveliness. They had perfectly arched brows, bluish-green eyes, Grecian noses, and lips curled to reveal captivating smiles. I spent countless hours staring at the photo. I loved showing it to people who knew them both to see if they could tell them apart. They never could.

But I could. They possessed different qualities. Gracie was nurturing; mother was inattentive. Gracie was a homebody, enjoying her role as wife and mother. Mother's interests lay outside the home, serving as president of several philanthropic organizations and preferring her friends' company to her children's.

Aunt Grace always greeted me on the front porch with a hug and a smile, making me feel wanted and loved. Her warmth was like being welcomed into a candle-lit café by a zealous Maître D'. Opening the door to my parents' home was as inviting as walking into a self-serve Horn and Hardart Automat.

One day, in January of 1950, a few months before the dreaded phone call, I stopped to see Aunt Grace. She answered the door in a state of excitement, threw her arms around me, and danced me into the house. "Did you hear the new song, Joanie? It's so funny. You've got to hear it." She skipped to the Magnavox console and held up a record jacket and waved it about. "This is it," she said. Then very gingerly took the 78rpm vinyl out of its paper sleeve. Circling her fingers carefully around the edges so as not to smudge the record, she placed it on the phonograph and turned up the volume.

Ray Bolger and Ethel Merman sang *Dearie*, a song that tested each other's memory. Ray asked Ethel if she remembered events such as the music played by the Sousa band, Chowder parties on July 4th, and Henry Ford before he invented the car. When Ethel answered *yes*, Ray would croon, "Well, Dearie, you're much older than I." Then Ethel asked Ray if he remembered Keystone movies, Coogan and Chaplin, Orville Wright flying Kittyhawk, and Mrs. O'Leary's cow that started the Chicago fire. Ray answered *yes*, and Ethel sang, "Well, Dearie, you're much older than I."

"Did you like it Sweetheart?" she asked. I could see she was eager for me to say yes. Her hands were in a clapping position.

"I did, Aunt Grace. I did. I liked it very much."

She clapped. "Would you like to hear it again?"

I nodded as she laughed and dropped the needle back on the record. *Who is Sousa?* I wondered. *Who's Mrs. O'Leary?* The melody was lively and fun, but there were so many strange names in the song that I didn't know: Coogan and Chaplin, Orville Wright and Kittyhawk.

Aunt Grace swayed and clapped in time to the music, and giggled every time Bing sang, *You're much older than I.* I never remember seeing her as bubbly and energetic as she was that winter day. (Years later, I was told by an aunt that Gracie had a drinking problem. Could she have been tipsy the day I found such joy being with her?)

Playing that record became a ritual over the next few months, until I left for camp. She explained the meaning of the words I didn't know and we sang the song together. Her happiness was contagious. I pointed at her and laughed as I sang out, "You're much older than I."

*****

How could a person as beautiful and loving as Aunt Grace die? She couldn't. Mother was wrong. She would not die. I felt that all I had to do was pray and truly believe that she would live and God would answer my prayers. I closed my eyes, recapturing the smiling face of Aunt Grace as she sang, "You're much older than I."

"Joanie, are you still there?" My eyes popped open. I looked around the room, glanced at the phone in my hand as I realized I was still in Miss Anne's office and Mother was on the other end of the receiver.

"Sorry, I was just thinking about Aunt Grace. Will you pray with me, Mother?"

"Oh sweetheart," she sighed into the phone. "Our prayers are not always answered. I had Anne put you on the phone instead of your sister because I know how much you and Aunt Grace love each other. Please tell Peppi that I called. We'll talk more when Dad and I arrive tomorrow for visiting day. We're bringing Salty. That should make you feel better." Hugging our dog would certainly lift my spirits. I was happy that Mother regarded my relationship with Aunt Grace as a highly significant alliance. We ended with the standards. "I love you," "Take care" and "I'll see you tomorrow."

I ran to the cabin quickly. I kept my head lowered as I hurried along to avoid eye contact with anyone. I didn't want to talk about Aunt Grace. I was much too upset and I had a lot of praying to do. I stretched out on my bunk bed as my mind flooded with memories. I thought of how I cried at age eight when my cat Tex died and about the time my grandfather David passed away at 84. Yet no one seemed too upset about it.

The dinner gong sounded but I ignored it. I was focused on my Uncle Lenny who was fourteen years old when I was born. I never got a chance to know him. I was three when he was drafted into the army in 1943 and six when he came home and moved back in with Aunt Grace. He had been living with her ever since their mother died in 1935 when he was ten.

My connection and love for Lenny was based on what my mother often told me. "You remind me so much of Uncle Lenny," she would say. "You're tall and thin and have his beautiful hazel eyes, and wonderful wide smile." Then tittering, she'd add, "Unfortunately, you also have his ungainly gait."

After his return from the war, Lenny went to work for my father, and Gracie and Mother arranged a gathering of young men and women for Lenny to meet. That is where he met Sarah Hollander. They dated for a year, got engaged and married in 1947. I didn't attend the wedding. My thoughts are hazy on the subject as to why, muddled between not wanting to go or being encouraged not to go because I was eight-years-old and thought too young to attend.

Their daughter, Alix, was born in 1949 and was only eight months old when Lenny died of a heart attack. He was twenty-five. I remember how everyone cried, and how Mother and Aunt Grace never seemed quite the same afterward. They were like the mercury in a thermometer which suddenly drops to zero on the first day of a cold snap, then rises little by little, degree by degree, as the months go by, but never reaches the warmth it once had before that first day of the frost.

Later, after the evening activities, I could hear my bunkmates' lively voices singing and laughing their way toward the cabin. They charged in, letting the screen door bang closed, and rushed toward the bathroom without so much as a glance in my direction, except for my hometown best friend, Barbara, who stopped by my bed. I felt guilty as I ignored her and pretended to be asleep. Barbara and I had been friends since birth.

"Joan," she whispered. "Are you all right?"

"Mmmmmm!" I moaned.

"Will you tell me what's wrong in the morning?" she asked. I shook my head. Barbara told the other girls that I was sick and that they should quiet down. They did.

Our counselor, Beth, came in a few minutes later and walked directly over to me. She whispered in my ear. "Miss Anne told me what happened. Try to sleep peacefully. I'm sure all will be well." She kissed my cheek and then announced, "Fifteen minutes till lights out. Let's move it along, girls; quietly please!"

That night I lay awake, desperately trying to believe that Aunt Grace would live. I knew it was my responsibility to plead for her recovery and that my love and prayers would keep her alive. I held images of Aunt Grace dancing to her favorite record and thanked God for making her my Aunt. I promised Him that I would always be honest and good if she recovered.

My positive thoughts were constantly disrupted by the fear that she would die, leaving my prayers unanswered. The night seemed endless as I struggled to stay firm, just the way Jacob did when he wrestled with the angel as told in the Bible. He held on to the angel until the break of day and the angel blessed him. I was determined to hold on to the certainty of Gracie's life until the light broke through the windows.

As the night wore on, I sensed I was losing the battle with the positive "angel thoughts." *What if she died in spite of my prayers? What would I do without her?*

Mother said she was very, very sick. My prayers must save her. But they won't, I know they won't. Yes, they will. I know they will. No they won't. No they won't. No they won't. No they won't. I wept softly until at last I fell asleep.

Before long we were awakened by the sound of the bugle. Parents Day! The morning sunshine put hope back into my heart. I really believed that my aunt was alive and well. Beth began to hurry us out of bed. Her tall, slender frame and muscular body reminded me of a greyhound prancing toward the starting gate eager to win the race. In her usual energetic manner she barked, "Take your showers, make your beds, and clean this place up! The bunk must look ship-shape before your parents arrive at 11:00." She smiled and winked at me.

A few hours later my sister Peppi and I ran toward our parents as they came down the road from the soccer field parking lot. Salty, a three-year-old West Highland White Terrier, pulled the leash right out of Mother's hand. We bent down with outstretched arms. He bounced from one of us to the other, licking our faces, wagging his tail, and rolling over for us to scratch his tummy.

"Let's take Salty for a little walk down the hill," Mother said, standing me up. My Father took Peppi's hand and led her up the hill. As we walked, Mom put her arm around me and pulled me closer.

We talked about the weather, about camp, about the food, about everything but Aunt Grace's battle with pneumonia.

I finally asked, "Is Gracie home from the hospital?" She squinted down at me with a finger to her lips. She opened her mouth. "Ummm," she said, and stopped. She kneeled down so we were almost eye to eye. "Sweetheart, I don't know how to tell you, it's so hard to find the right words, but Aunt Grace passed away during the night."

All I could do was hold onto my mother as I sobbed. Aunt Grace had died, and I knew why! The power of grief and guilt paralyzed my moving and speaking. My brain was a jumble of words – failure – weakling – murderer. I wanted to confess, but the words would not come. *How could I tell her that my tears of sorrow were overlaid with cries of remorse? My awful secret—a secret so dreadful and so unspeakable—that it must be sealed in my heart and soul forever. If I had not let myself think, even for a moment, that she would die, she would have lived. It was I who killed my aunt.* I trembled with the knowledge of my crime, but my lips could not utter the awful truth.

When the self-incrimination ended, I calmed down enough to feel Mother shaking. I looked up and saw her wet eyes and runny nose. She smiled and handed me a tissue and used one herself. Then we headed for the cafeteria where Father and Peppi joined us after their discussion of Gracie's death.

I hadn't told Peppi about Mother's phone call. I'd completely forgotten. I reasoned that it didn't matter anyway as her relationship with Gracie was more casual. Peppi was closer to Uncle Lenny and continued to see Sarah and their baby, Alix, whom she adored.

After lunch, Mother and Father walked us back to the Cadillac and opened the trunk. It was filled with games, comic books, cookies, candy, and gum, which we were to share with our bunk mates. By the time we said goodbye to our parents, all the excitement of the day left me more subdued by exhaustion than by grief, and I slept peacefully that night.

In the morning I woke up feeling like a wriggling earthworm cut in two – half of me numb and deadened to emotion, the other half struggling to stay alive and return to my carefree days.

The news had spread, and throughout that day campers and counselors expressed condolences. I managed to squeak out a few words of thanks, but each well-wisher received a flood of tears. During the next four weeks of camp, the activities felt less enjoyable, the food less tasty, the nights less restful, and the days less cheerful. I began to spend all my free time in the grass-covered fields, watching the clouds sail by, nursing the wound that would not heal.

My own thermometer had hit its freezing point.

*****

Aunt Grace's death altered my outlook on life. Yet 1950 had begun at a time when my world seemed ordinary and predictable. That changed on May 29, when our family was preparing to go to the club for the pool opening. Just before we were about to leave, I ran to the bathroom and came out crying. My first menstrual cycle had arrived, and I knew I would be banned from swimming. I had to sit by the side of the pool and watch the rest of the kids having fun or lie on the lounge until I got so hot that I splashed myself with water. One thing I didn't do that day was smile. I ran to Aunt Grace that evening to express my disappointment. She hugged me and said, "Congratulations!"

"Congratulations?" I asked.

"Sweetheart, you're a woman now. I saw it the moment you walked in." She walked me to the mirror. "Look at yourself. See how shapely you've become?

"None of my friends look like this. I'm awkward."

"Just stand tall like the magazine models and show the undeveloped girls what they have to look forward to." I blushed and giggled. She stroked my cheek. "Your complexion is like peaches and cream. In no time at all, you'll knock those boys dead." I walked home practicing good posture.

At the end of June, I was on a train to Woodlands camp, not realizing I'd never see Aunt Grace again.

*****

When the summer ended, I was in the throes of pubescence and mourning the loss of my confidante and protector. I felt as useless as a mound of dirt without a flag pole. I devoted that autumn to biking, roller skating, seeing friends, watching television, and keeping up my usual "C" average. Nothing in my everyday life seemed changed except the loss of Gracie, which coated everything with a film of sorrow. Mother hovered over Gracie's youngest, Jimmy. I played with him every day after school. I bought him roller skates with my allowance, as if this could make up for the loss of his Mother. Jimmy sat on the front steps as I attached the skates to the bottom of his shoes and tightened the clamps with a skate key. He put his hands into mine and I helped him to his feet. Slowly, I began to walk backwards along the sidewalk as he rolled along. Once he caught his balance, I said, "Now pick up one foot and hold it as long as you can. Good. Now put it down and pick up the other." It took several spills, a few bouts of laughter, and a scraped knee, but he learned to skate that very day.

Friday night dinners were reserved for Harmon, Jimmy, and their father, Don. Father and Don always had a scotch and soda in the living room before we sat down to eat. Peppi and Harmon sat and talked in her room, and Jimmy and I played board games in the den until the dinner bell rang. Our housekeeper, Hedy, served her famous prime ribs, roasted potatoes, and lemon meringue pie for dessert. An undertone of pretense accompanied the chit-chat and laughter. Aunt Grace's death was never mentioned.

Mother surprised us that winter with tickets for the Rockettes at Radio City Music Hall. As soon as we arrived home after seeing the show, Peppi and I threw our arms around each other and practiced high kicking. On New Year's Eve, as our parents headed out the door to a party, Peppi pleaded for us to stay up until midnight. We sat in front of the television with a bowl of popcorn and a dish of ice cream watching the broadcast from Times Square, counting the seconds as the ball dropped, turning 1950 into 1951. We made our New Year's Eve wishes. I wished that Aunt Grace were still alive.

In February, Father made an offer on a house Mother wanted him to buy from the time they moved to Paterson in 1934. It was located two blocks from our current home and situated between the same two avenues. Mother screamed and jumped up and down like a little girl the night Father brought home the contract. Preparations for moving started immediately with fabrics, paint chips, and catalogue clippings scattered all over the house.

Harmon graduated from high school that June, and worked at the country club until he left for the University of Indiana. Peppi had the choice of going to camp that summer or working. She chose work at a day camp. This time I was given a choice of camps.

My mother's best friend was Barbara's mother, Anne, and as such we went to the same camp each year. So Barbara and I consulted and agreed on Camp Akiba in Stroudsburg, Pennsylvania, in the heart of the Poconos. Although most of our camp life was spent at Akiba, occasionally Mother or Anne heard about a great camp advertised on the radio, and sent us up to Vermont, New Hampshire, or Maine for the summer. Half the Jewish families in Paterson sent their children to Akiba, so I felt comfortable at this camp on the Delaware Water Gap.

While Peppi and I were away, our parents moved into the new home and hired Hedy as our new housekeeper. This Georgian Colonial home featured an oval, high-ceilinged vestibule with a spiral staircase, above which hung a crystal chandelier. We not only had a dining room, but an eat-in kitchen and a breakfast room separated by a butler's pantry. The expansive backyard featured a patio that extended the length of the house, a fish pond surrounded by a rock garden, and a gazebo in which I spent many hours. I loved our new home, especially my bedroom which was twice the size as my old room.

When I was six, living in our home on 35th Street, the Sunshine family bought a house on 36th Street which bordered our property. There was a slight incline, jam-packed with foliage, between our two backyards. Through the kitchen window, Peppi spied a young girl, about my age, sucking her thumb and clinging to her mother while she pinned clothes on a circular, spinning clothes line. Peppi grabbed my hand and insisted we introduce ourselves to the new neighbors. We struggled through the heavy shrubbery, and arrived scratched and grazed onto a pristine lawn with a walk-in doll house. A slim girl with long straight hair looked up, startled. Peppi introduced us to the girl and her mother. When Jane and I became best friends, our parents shared the cost of a stairway to be built between our homes so that Jane and I wouldn't have to struggle through the shrubbery to play with one another. Jane used these stairs to pick me up each morning for our walk to school. After we moved to 37th Street, Jane still had to pick me up for school because we both knew that we would be late for school if she waited for me to fetch her.

Jane always had to hurry me along, finding my shoes, gathering together papers and books, and as the weather got progressively colder, sweaters, coats, gloves, and hats.

*****

I met Janice in 1952. She had just moved into the new house built on the adjacent corner. She rang my bell and introduced herself. Janice was two years younger than I, but we hit it off and soon became default friends. When either one of us had nothing to do, we'd seek each other out. One such day in September, I rang her doorbell and her brother, Rorry, answered the door.

42

"May I help you?" he asked. Janice told me she had a brother, but I had not met him before. He was so handsome.

"Uh, ummm, uh, is Janice home?"

"No, I'm sorry. She's visiting with our cousin. I was just on my way to meet her." He smiled, and I was hooked.

"Tell her Joan was looking for her. I live next door. "

"I know. I've seen you from my bedroom window." He grabbed a jacket from a hook and closed the door. We walked down the steps to the sidewalk.

"I guess I'll see you around then, Joan."

"Uh, yeah, sure." I said, too muddled to say more.

"Bye now," Rorry said, and walked away without a backward glance.

As I watched him go, I yearned to make him mine and brazenly chased after him for the next four years to no avail.

My liberation from having to go to summer camp came in 1953 at age 14. This was none too soon, as I would be entering high school in the fall and considered myself too old to be a camper. Instead, I went with my parents to Las Vegas and California. Peppi graduated high school that June and was signed up with Teen Tours to travel out west to the National Parks with a stop in San Francisco. We planned to meet Peppi in San Francisco.

The day after we arrived at LAX airport, a friend of my parents took us sightseeing in Los Angeles, which included a stop at the Beverly Wilshire Hotel. Ed Sullivan was hosting his daughter's wedding reception. Many of the guests wandered into the reception area from the ballroom where we were standing. Mother encouraged me to get autographs from the stars she recognized: George Burns and Gracie Allen, Bob Hope, Vic Damone, Zsa Zsa Gabor, Dean Martin, Jerry Lewis, and Elizabeth Taylor, who was wearing the iconic poodle skirt of the 1950s.

The next day we visited a fair at the Farmer's Market. A graphologist was in a booth analyzing peoples' handwriting in order to identify their psychological state and personality traits. He wanted to see Mother's current writing as well as a selection from her past. I watched as mother wrote a paragraph and her signature on a piece of paper. She searched her purse, found an address book, and handed it to him. The man studied her jottings for some time as we stood in front of his table. He placed the paper on the counter and pointed to the script. "I consider slant, size, spacing, and other details to analyze hand writing," he said. "I see that you're outgoing, sociable, openhearted and helpful, with excellent organizational skills. You dislike confrontation. You have a strong need to feel secure."

Mother laughed. "That sounds very right to me!"

"I also see that recently some traumatic event has saddened you." Her laughter turned to tears. He placed the address book next to the paper. He pointed out the contrast between the former and current squiggles which had altered enough to expose her innermost feelings.

We walked away from the experience in silence. I didn't know what to say. I was afraid to mention Aunt Grace's death. Mother's tears surprised me. Silence and repression didn't stop the trauma of her death from erupting. Mother hadn't forgotten Gracie, as I had thought. Being reminded of her made me feel apprehensive, although I didn't know why. Time had allowed my initial devastation to slip into the realm of the unconscious. I was cognizant only of the fact that she was gone.

The California trip brought a second bout of tears to mother while watching the film *Never Let Me Go* with Gene Tierney. "Why were you crying?" I asked as we exited the theater.

"Gene Tierney reminded me of Gracie. She looked just like her," Mother said. This time I felt comforted by her tears. A union of sorrow embraced us. I held her hand as we walked and felt disappointed that I hadn't seen Grace's face in Gene. Perhaps Mother perceived a quality in the actress that wasn't apparent to me. I supposed it was because my focus was on Clark Gable.

On the eighth night of our trip, we packed the car and drove to Las Vegas for a few days. We had to travel at night because it was too hot to drive during the day. Mother and I spent four days at the pool while Father played golf. We'd have dinner together at night and see a show. Although I was too young to be allowed in the casinos, Mother said I could play the slot machines and gave me a roll of nickels. I had fun until a guard in a black suit kicked me out.

Because I was not allowed into the casino anymore, Father bought me a bank shaped like a slot machine. I dropped a coin in and pulled the handle. It dropped down, accompanied by the spin of cherries, oranges, and apples, and with the same resounding clink as the real thing. Father promised to share his winnings with me from the night before to fill the bank. The next morning I opened my eyes to find that there was no money beside the bank. In fact, there was no bank. I laughed. I knew they were playing a trick on me. They must have lost the night before and wanted me to pay my share. I couldn't wait until they woke up so I could pretend I was upset and scared that someone stole my bank. I never felt closer to my parents than I did that morning.

Once back in California we drove up the coast to Santa Barbara and Carmel. We drove inland to Yosemite, before circling back to San Francisco where we met Peppi. No sooner had she appeared at the hotel restaurant than an argument broke out between her and Father. Most likely it was about her lackadaisical appearance or her outspoken behavior.

"One of these days I'm going to disown that girl," Father said after Peppi abruptly left her half eaten dessert and rejoined her travel group.

"Calm down," Mother said. "You'll give yourself a stroke."

"Why does she always have to be so ornery?" Father raised his eyes as if he were pleading with God for an answer.

My parents didn't hesitate to voice their annoyance at Peppi in front of me.

"She's been that way forever," Mother said. "Don't you think it's time to ignore her rebellious behavior?" She took her last sip of coffee.

As I listened to my parents argue, I realized Peppi was the catalyst that turned our happy trio into an inharmonious quartet, not unlike the dining room battles of our early youth. Why had it taken me so long to see this?

It was the first time I saw Father and Mother as more than just parents and realized that they had worries and fears of their own, sometimes with differing points of view. My perspective about our family dynamics changed and broadened from that point forward, relieving me of a lot of frustration.

*****

Rorry was not the first or the last boy from whom I sought love. Back in the spring of 1950, the year of transformation, when I was in sixth grade, Sean dragged me into the boy's locker room. I pretended to protest. He grabbed me by the shoulders, pulled me toward him, bent me backwards as they do in the movies, and gave me my first kiss. I loved it. My friend Sheila met him first and introduced him to Roz, who introduced him to me. They also liked Sean, so I became third in line for his affection. The four of us spent a lot of time together, and Sean spent a lot of time with each of us separately.

In those days grammar school went from kindergarten to eighth grade in the same building. The higher the grade, the more respect and admiration you received from your peers. Those younger than I, who experienced middle school, tell stories of how they were tormented if they deviated in the slightest from what was considered the norm. By today's standards, we were quite innocent and hadn't reached the sophistication and worldliness the kids of today have by sixth grade. Otherwise, I might have avoided the effects of what happened next.

The day I was convinced that Sean liked me best was the day he and my eight-year-old cousin Jimmy came to visit at the same time. We played a few board games together and then I suggested that Jimmy find Peppi and see what she was doing. He didn't want to do that. So we played a few rounds of hide and seek. Jimmy was *it* on the third round, and Sean and I hid in the attic closet where we hoped we wouldn't be found for a long time. We sat on the floor. Sean put his arm around my shoulder and told me how he jumped the ocean waves at Seaside Heights and how he pinched coins from vending machines. He described, in detail, each item he bought with the money. I listened intently and wished I could go with him to the Jersey Shore. He kissed me gently on the lips between every adventure story. Sean handed me a flattened coin with his name printed on it as a gift. I kissed him when he gave me the keepsake. All went well until Peppi opened the door abruptly with Jimmy at her side and threatened to tell Mother I was necking in the closet. I had no idea what necking meant or why it was wrong. Jimmy was being a pest, and we just wanted to get rid of him for a while. Peppi pulled me out of the closet and told Sean to go home. I yelled at Jimmy for being a tattle-tale and he ran downstairs.

I thought that Peppi was angry about the way I treated Jimmy, and I felt guilty over what I had done. Peppi dragged me down the steps after him, but whereas Jimmy went all the way to the first floor, Peppi pushed me into Mother's room where we found her sitting on the side of her bed talking on the phone. Mother looked at us quizzically. "I'll call you back," she said, and hung up.

"Do you know what Joan was doing?" Peppi said, and sat down next to Mother. "She was in the closet with Sean, *necking*." She folded her arms in front of her.

I stood before them as an accused in front of a jury. "We were just playing hide and seek," I said.

"You were necking," Peppi said.

"We were just talking," I said.

"Joan, be careful." Mother warned. "Boys are after only one thing. They don't have to love you to enjoy your hugs and kisses."

I liked when Sean kissed me and it felt perfectly lovely having his arm around me. If that's what necking is, I guess I like what the boys like. Maybe I was supposed to be a boy. Mother always said Father wanted one. I wonder if something went wrong at birth or got mixed up before I was born. I was too frightened to express these thoughts to Mother and didn't dare say anything about it in front of Peppi. I pondered the idea for days before I asked Roz if she liked being kissed. She did! Then I asked Sheila. She did, too. I reasoned that it was only Mother and Peppi who didn't like being kissed and let the subject drop, although it had a sustaining influence on my psyche.

In mid-May, I felt as tall and ungainly as the Scarecrow in the Wizard of Oz with a brain to match. Mother walked into the den where I was sprawled out on the couch watching television. She took one look at my sour look and out-of-focus expression, and asked, "What's wrong, Joan? Why aren't you your usual upbeat self?"

"I feel depressed and bloated," I said. She turned off the television.

"Do you feel feverish?" she asked.

"No," I said. "But I'm feeling jumbly and weird."

"What's going on?" she asked, and pushed my legs gently back to give herself room to sit down.

"It's hard to explain. I feel sad like something's missing in my life."

"Like what?" She asked and placed her hand on my head.

"I feel like crying all the time, but I don't know why."

"Maybe you should call a friend," Mother sighed, and brushed my hair back.

"I don't want to be with anybody. I don't like any of my friends. In fact, I feel like I'm all alone in the world," I said, moving her hand away.

"How could you feel all alone with a mother, father, and sister running around the house? Not to mention Hedy, who's always underfoot?" She smiled at this joke, as if any of us could ever be bothered by our beloved housekeeper. "What about Jane and Barbara, two of your dearest friends? They love you."

"I know, it sounds silly, it's just that…." I gave Mother a gentle nudge with my knees, indicating that I wanted to sit up. "I wish…I wish I had my own boyfriend," I said. "Someone special to love and who will love only me."

"I'm sure someday you will. You're only twelve, you have time. You don't want to get married tomorrow, do you?"

I thought that was funny, but I refused to laugh. I wasn't finished feeling sorry for myself. "Nobody's going to love me. I'm ugly and dumb."

"Don't be silly. You are not ugly and dumb. You're just as pretty as your friends, if not prettier."

That's when Mother gave me her advice on how to attract boys into my life.

She advised, "Dress nicely and always be well groomed. Boys like girls who are easy going, enthusiastic, and good sports. Be attentive to their every word. If a boy talks about baseball or football, express interest. Boys like to talk about themselves. They like to solve all your problems and feel they must be in charge of everything. However, you can turn that around and secretly be in control yourself if you learn how to handle boys. All it takes is to make them believe that they were the source of the idea, the advice, or the solution."

This confused me. Was she now encouraging me to seek the attention of boys? What happened to, *they don't have to love you to hug and kiss you?* Should I attract them, but not hug and kiss them? How will I know if I am truly loved? It is something I wanted more than anything. Marilyn Monroe was loved by everyone, it seemed. I wanted to be her.

I decided to watch my mother's interaction with Father more carefully to learn how to *handle* boys well enough for one of them to fall in love with me for real. The search to be loved was on.

When I was promoted to seventh grade, Sean graduated from grammar school and moved on to high school. He no longer took an interest in me (or Roz or Sheila), and we bonded together in our loneliness. It wasn't that any of us missed Sean per se; we had long ago understood that none of us would get his individual attention. What we missed was having someone to call a boyfriend. We were three of the tallest girls in our class, towering over even the eighth-grade boys. Finding romance – our top priority at our school – was out of the question, and we had nowhere else to search. Mother's suggestions would have to wait.

*****

Meeting Rorry gave me my first opportunity to practice Mother's advice. We met when Rorry was a freshman in high school. He traveled by bus to Montclair Academy, a private school. I was in eighth grade and still walking to school with Jane. This resulted in days when I had school and Rorry did not. When I was home and Rorry had school, I'd put Salty on his leash and watch from my parent's window for Rorry to leave for school. As soon as I saw him, I'd rush downstairs, head out the door, and pretend it was coincidence that we met.

One glorious Indian-summer evening, during the first two weeks of our acquaintance, Salty was scratching on the front door announcing that he had to go out. "Salty needs a walk," I yelled. "Can someone take him? My favorite show is about to start."

55

"I'm doing homework," Peppi yelled back.

"I'm on the phone," Mother shouted.

Grudgingly, I leashed the dog and walked out the front door. Rorry was passing by on his way to Ben and Bob's, a local candy store and hang out. This accidental meeting was the first time we spent time together alone. We walked to the corner, but instead of him going down the hill to the store, he stayed with me as I crossed the street and headed into the park. I was in heaven! We walked the dog around a bit and then sat on the grass and continued our conversation. I used to remember what we chatted about, but it is now gone from memory. But I do remember sitting by Rorry's side, drinking in his every word, intoxicated by his mere presence, fully addicted to his good looks and charm.

Around 10:00 p.m., I heard Father calling me. I didn't answer, but released Salty's leash from my hand. He ran directly to Father. "Where's Joan?" he asked the dog. Luckily, dogs can't talk and I was able to continue what turned out to be the only magical moment I ever had with Rorry. I didn't want the evening to end but soon began feeling guilty about worrying Father. Rorry walked me to the front door, kissed me gently, with lips closed, and left me dreaming of hopes for the future.

Rorry's feelings for me were elusive. One day he'd be approachable and jovial, another day, cold and critical. He reminded me of a cat who sidles up to you when it wants attention, ignores you when it doesn't, and at all times is totally indifferent to your presence.

Some days Rorry genuinely seemed happy to see me and greeted me warmly. He usually did most of the talking, and when he did, I practiced Mother's theory of *attentiveness*. Not that it was difficult; after all, I was in love, wasn't I?

One day as I tagged along to his bus stop, he interrupted me mid-sentence to tell me he wished I was more like my cousin, Connie.

"What do you mean?" I asked.

"She's terrific. She's so beautiful with a perfect nose. *(I had a big nose.)* Do you know she's in the top of her class? *(I was somewhere under the 50% mark.)* She's got two boys fighting over her. *(I was having trouble getting this one to even look at me.)* She's such a joy to be with."

He didn't express all those sentiments on that one day and perhaps not exactly in that manner. But he did ask that question, and listening to him rave about Connie was, after all, part of being attentive. Over time, his admiration for his cousin played havoc with my self-esteem. She was beautiful, and had an air of independence about her which bordered on superiority. Her family had a pool in their backyard which was enviable. Connie invited Rorry and me to an evening swim party. Although the evening atmosphere was warm and inviting, Connie was cold, and most of the guests were unapproachable. Nevertheless, I continued my pursuit to secure his love, knowing I could never be like his cousin Connie.

B.F. Skinner would have been proud of me. It would have proven his theory that *intermittent reinforcement increases resistance to the extinction of behavior.* In other words, Rorry's sporadic acceptance of my advances kept me forever trying to recreate that evening of joy and serenity in the park. Rorry acted as the experimenter, feeding me just enough kindness, every now and again, to ensure repeated attempts for his affection.

I began to see myself as an unlucky charm in the game of life. For instance, Eastside High School had an excellent reputation, but seeing it from inside, it failed to live up to its high standing. I was convinced that it was my attendance that caused the downward trend. I found the extra-curricular activities, at which my sister excelled, disorganized and boring. Was it me? Eastside had sororities and I pledged for one of the top two. After initiation, I found it lacked the luster of its status. Did I bring down their shine? Girls I befriended, because of their perceived integrity, began to show disagreeable personality traits and insecurities. They appeared catty and often malicious. Was it my mere presence that caused them to act this way? No matter what avenue I traveled, disillusionments confronted me. Friends disappointed, boys offended, teachers reprimanded, and parents disciplined.

Outwardly, I was the proverbial Good Time Charlie – outgoing, amenable, full of jokes and laughter – demonstrating talents acquired from Mother's lessons on how a woman succeeds in life.

My friends would ask, "Would you like to go to *fill in the blank*?" Whether it was cruising, partying, shopping, or hanging out in the park, my answer was always the same – *Yes!* I was still following those gusts of wind.

Inwardly, I viewed myself as a Nash Rambler in a flock of Cadillacs, my self-esteem buried beneath layers of repressed memories and false pretenses.

*****

My sixteenth birthday party was held at the Meadowbrook, a popular nightclub in Cedar Grove, which attracted the big bands of the day. I invited

59

Rorry to be my date and was ecstatic when he accepted. I have a picture of me sitting in a chair with Rorry perched on the arm and smiling into the camera. I'm dressed in a spaghetti strapped, yellow and brown floral print with a full skirt and two crinolines underneath. A corsage sits lopsided on my shoulder. I'm gazing into his face with such reverence you'd think I was a Catholic having an audience with the Pope.

I loved Rorry, but Rorry never declared any feelings for me, although at times he acted as if he cared. During one of those times, I took a silver dollar and had it split in half in a zigzag pattern so that each half would fit together to look like a solid coin, and put them on chains. I presented Rorry with one of them. He accepted the gift, but I have no recollection of him wearing it.

The high school sororities and fraternities sponsored dances. Each one entered one of their members to run for Queen or King of the dance. When I was seventeen, I was selected by my sorority to run for Queen. My boyfriend Michael, the president of the KATZ Fraternity, was my date.

To my surprise, Rorry showed up with his cousin to vote for me. At the end of the evening, I went to retrieve my picture on the entrance hall table, which was placed beside the picture of the contestant who won. Mine was missing. Someone had taken it. I doubted it was Michael. We had been dating for months, and he carried a picture of me in his wallet.

Was it Rorry? I hoped so. My fantasies surrounding this mysterious disappearance centered on Rorry taking my picture, framing it, and keeping it on his dresser. I imagined he couldn't express his love because his cousin wouldn't like it. He was waiting until she left for college, and then he would appear at my door, carrying the picture, and express his undying love.

At the start of my senior year of high school, I was still dating Michael when Rorry invited me to join his family for a trip to Vermont to attend homecoming weekend at Middlebury College. Now I was sure he loved and missed me. Without saying anything to Michael, I accepted the invitation. Mother was somewhat apprehensive about my going, but when I told her that we'd be driving up with his parents and sister, she agreed and helped me pick out my clothes and pack my suitcase.

Most of our time was spent with Rorry's family and friends. We were only alone when we drove to his fraternity party. He was aloof, without much to say. He introduced me to his friends. We sat on a couch for a while, until he arose with the pretense of getting us something to eat, and didn't come back until it was time to leave. A boy came over to talk to me. I told him how I was being ignored and that I hated Rorry. The boy was sympathetic, offering understanding and companionship. I didn't accept his offer to take me back to the hotel, and I knew I didn't hate Rorry.

*****

Driving home, I sat in the back seat in silence, reviewing my relationship (or non-relationship) with Rorry. *What was going on?* My friend Debbie once said, "You know, Joan, you walk more like Rorry should, and he walks more like you should. I'm pretty sure he's queer." The probability of Rorry being gay seemed impossible at the time. Even Liberace wasn't that, just theatrical.

Years later someone confirmed that Rorry was gay. He was forced to hide his true nature from a world that ostracized homosexuality. How awful for him. Our on again, off again relationship was his attempt to see if he could be straight. Perhaps he told his friends at Middlebury that he had a hometown girlfriend to justify his lack of interest in the young co-eds and tried to prove it by having me make an appearance.

I blame my persistent love for Rorry on Rodgers and Hammerstein's *Carousel,* my first Broadway show. Mother bought tickets for the family to celebrate my eighth birthday, and thus began my fascination with theater—and my misperception of love. The moment the curtain went up, I was transported into the world of Julie and Billy. I lived each moment of the story along with the actors, identifying with Julie and making her love for Billy the foundation on which my idea of true love was based: once you find the boy you love, you don't stop loving him no matter how he treats you. I took the words of the song "What's the Use of Wond'rin" to heart.

So, when he wants your kisses

You will give them to the lad,

And anywhere he leads you, you will walk.

And anytime he needs you,

You'll go runnin there like mad.

You're his girl and he's your feller

And all the rest is talk.

✶✶✶✶✶

A few days after the disastrous trip to Vermont, I received an envelope in the mail which contained Rorry's halved silver dollar without a word of empathy or regret. My thermometer, once again, hit zero. I wished Aunt Grace were here to comfort me. I sat on my bed listening to songs of unrequited love. I wanted to cry, but the tears wouldn't come.

"Dinner's ready," Hedy called from the bottom of the staircase.

"I'm not hungry," I yelled back.

Mother was at my door in a minute. "Are you sick?" she asked.

"No, I'm just not hungry."

"You, not hungry for dinner—I don't believe it," she said standing directly over me.

I handed her the envelope. "Oh," she said. "I understand."

The tears flowed. "Joan, I promise, you'll fall in love again. Rorry is not the only fish in the sea, you know? Boys are always calling the house for you." TablThat was true, and I dated any boy who asked me out whether I liked him or not.

Mother sat by my side until I finished crying. "You know what we're going to do?" she asked. I shook my head. "We're going to call Dr. Lewin and talk to him about a nose job."

"Really?" I said. I wanted one ever since Rorry asked me to be more like his cousin.

"Really," Mother replied. "Now wash your face and come down for dinner."

What an ideal remedy for a broken heart. I was delighted, even smiling and joining the family for dinner.

Mother made an appointment with Dr. Lewin, a plastic surgeon recommended by a friend. "You've come at the right time," he said, "I don't like to do rhinoplasty on a young lady under the age of seventeen." As he took pictures and measurements of my facial features, he spoke softly, asking me questions about my life. His kindness and attention made me feel so at ease that I had no fear on the day of the surgery, although I can't say that I felt the same way when he visited me in the recovery room.

On his follow up visit, Dr. Lewin changed the bandage to a lighter one which exposed the tip of my nose. I thought I looked like Kim Novak, and constantly admired myself in the mirror until the bandages were removed. I no longer looked like

Kim, but the winter holidays, with its myriad festivities, kept my spirits flying. However, by my 18th birthday in April 1957, when nothing in my life seemed to change, I started going to bed early every night. Jane was back waking me up every morning for school. I threw on my clothes without washing up and grabbed a Hershey bar for breakfast. I stopped seeing friends, focused only on television, and often fell asleep until dinner. When Mother tried to help by asking what was wrong, I'd say "Nothing," or "Just leave me alone." I was finding it hard to deal with life's uncertainty. I wanted autonomy, yet needed authority. I wanted control, yet lacked confidence. I wanted love, but felt unlovable.

"I need a psychiatrist," I announced one night at the dinner table.

"Don't be ridiculous!" Father responded, with a mouth full of food.

"They're a bunch of quacks!" Mother added, waving her hand dismissively.

"No they aren't! I want you to ask Dr. Schulman to recommend a psychiatrist – or…" I played with my mashed potatoes. "I'll ask the school nurse to find mc onc," I taunted.

"You most certainly will not." They spoke in unison.

"All they do is blame everything on the parents," Mother said in panic.

"No they don't. They'll help me. I'm upset and confused and I need to figure things out." I pushed my plate away and plunked my head down on the table.

"Can't you just tell us what's troubling you, dear?" Mother asked as she reached over and patted my shoulder. I shrugged her hand aside and sat up straight.

"I don't know what's troubling me. If I did, I wouldn't need a psychiatrist!" The frustration in my voice was hard to miss.

"For God's sake," Father said, putting an end to the confrontation. "Let her go for a few weeks to get it out of her system." He slammed his coffee cup down and walked away from the table, shaking his head and muttering, "What the hell she needs a psychiatrist for, I'll never know."

*****

In my third month of therapy, I was lying on Dr. Milo Shapiro's couch, doing a free association exercise, babbling about whatever came to mind, when the memory of Aunt Grace's death suddenly surfaced from the depths of my unconscious. My hands felt icy and my body trembled. All at once, I was at camp on that ill-fated day with my arms around my mother, gripping her waist ten times tighter than a super-control girdle. The details were remarkably clear. The feelings of grief and guilt were so vivid that I was both startled and fascinated by the experience. I felt like Alice falling down the rabbit hole with memories surfacing faster than I could verbalize. Heart-wrenching sobs accompanied the visualizations. I came through the experience with a combined sense of fatigue and exhilaration.

Over the next several weeks we explored this early childhood wounding and how it affected my outlook on life and my self-image. Delving into the past was the highlight of my week. I began to understand how my unconscious thoughts were the basis for my actions and caught a glimpse of why I thought myself a jinx. The process of therapy intrigued me. I loved how talking about a topic that seemed unimportant always brought something significant to light.

A major benefit from the therapeutic work was that I was able to broach the subject of Aunt Grace with Mother. We sat at the kitchen table as I recreated my experience on the psychiatrist's couch.

She listened intently without saying a word. When I finished the story, she said, "I was just trying to let you down easily, Joan. I had no idea you would react this way. I thought I was doing the right thing."

"I know you didn't mean to hurt me, Mom, and I'm not blaming you," I said, fully aware of her fear. "I just wanted to share my insight with you."

"But you don't understand." She seemed visibly shaken. "You see, when I phoned you, Aunt Grace was already dead. I thought it would be better to break the news to you slowly." I must have had a startled expression on my face because she added, "Do you understand what I'm saying?"

I heard the words, I understood them, but the significance of what had been said did not immediately register.

"I'm sorry. I'm so terribly sorry," she muttered.

Luckily for both of us, the phone rang and I saw that Mother was uncertain about answering. I jumped from the chair, pointed toward the phone, nodded yes and leapt up the stairs. I took two steps at a time, causing a muscle cramp in my leg which forced me to sit on the landing and relax the spasm by pressing my fingers up and down the injured limb. I stayed in that position for quite a while, massaging the tension out as I searched my thoughts for meaning and understanding: all those years of repressed guilt, for what? Because a child believed her negative thinking could magically create tragedy! Because a young girl was afraid to speak up! Because something done out of kindness turned out to be the very opposite!

How did I feel about Mother's technique of "letting me down easily"? Hurt or angry? Could I forgive her? Did she deserve forgiving?

Mother and I bonded in California. Our interaction was easy and trouble free. The tears Mother shed in Los Angeles with the graphologist, the laughter over the missing coin bank in Las Vegas, and the lesson on family dynamics in San Francisco, brought us closer. Mother introduced me to theater, imparted her philosophy for a successful life, and was at hand when the loss of Rorry devastated me. Surely, Mother's revealing Gracie's death the way she did stemmed from a sense of love and protection. She acted from her highest sense of right. How could she be faulted for that? I couldn't wait to explore these thoughts and questions with Dr. Shapiro.

Bobbie pulled up to my house in her Chevy Bel Air convertible. "Hop in!" she said. Her father was a hair dresser and could afford to buy her a car. My father, a business magnate, refused to buy me one. I complained to Mother that not only Bobbie had a car, but Jane had one, too. She was given a choice of getting a car or a harp for her seventeenth birthday. Jane chose the harp and three months later got the car as well. "Why don't you give me a choice like that?" I asked. "All right," Mother said, "Do you want a harp or a violin?"

"Where are we going?" I asked Bobbie as I jumped into the shot gun seat.

"Doan's Diner," she said. Doan's was a favorite evening hangout for seniors with cars. The parking lot was packed and every table taken. Someone shouted, "Over here, Bobbie." We made our way to a large table filled with boys and squeezed into the booth. They were from the Italian section of town. Although they went to our school, I had never met them before. We ordered a Coke, hamburger, and fries, and hoped the boys would pick up the tab. They didn't. Nevertheless, we talked and joked and went home happy.

The next day at school, Bobbie ran over to me and said, "Bill wants to drive you home from school."

"Who's Bill?" I asked.

"Who's Bill! You sat next to him all last night talking."

"I did? I don't remember him."

"Joan, you are the pits. I mean, really! He wants to drive you home from school today."

"But I have no idea what he looks like."

"He's cute, about your height, has dark hair, a wicked smile, and he's wearing a red V-neck sweater. Meet him at the Market Street entrance. You can't miss him."

For the rest of the day I kept reminding myself: Bill – red sweater – Market Street entrance. He was standing at the bottom of the steps, leaning up against the banister, looking ever so cool. He *was* cute. Still, I didn't recognize him from the night before.

On the drive home, I learned all about Bill's football career at school. He was a linebacker. When I told him that I didn't know anything about the game, he willingly explained how it was played. I became an immediate fan and went to all the games, including the final one against Central High, which was held on Thanksgiving Day. Eastside won, and Bill insisted that I go with him to all the celebratory parties, where I sat on the sidelines and watched him bask in admiration and glory.

On Christmas, I was invited to Bill's home for dinner. I never saw so much food prepared for one meal. Minestrone soup, antipasto, pasta marinara, pasta with clams, lasagna, green beans, potatoes, fish, chicken, cookies, and pies. I fell in love with his parents and younger brother and visited the family often, even into my adult life.

Bill lifted a large package from under the tree. "Merry Christmas," he said, handing it to me and kissing me on the cheek.

"Should I open it now?" I asked.

Everyone laughed. "Of course, it's a Christmas gift!" I tried to keep the Santa Claus and reindeer paper intact as I opened the present. Bill reached over and ripped it apart. It was a black leather wrap around car coat.

That night, when I showed it to Mother, she asked, "Are you sleeping with him?"

"No!" I said.

"Well, that is quite a gift to give a girl who's not."

I explained that Bill's mother was a garment worker in a coat factory and got the coat for cost.

"Oh," she said.

I felt unjustly accused. Why would she think I'd do that? I knew I was supposed to wait until I got married before having intercourse; boys wanted their wives to be virgins. Mother started asking questions: Where are you going? With whom? When will you be home? The distrust weighed on my mind. I thought back to a time before Thanksgiving when Bill came to call. My father answered the door. "Should you be going out tonight?" he asked Bill. "Don't you have a football game tomorrow?"

"Yes, but I like to be with Joan. She calms me down." Bill replied.

"Well, just be sure she *calms* you down." My father retorted. We all laughed. Now I wondered if he, too, doubted my virginity. I continued to reject Bill's advances. Then, on a delightfully warm spring night, in the back seat of his car, I reasoned, *if I'm going to be accused of a crime, I might as well commit it.* To say the experience was dissatisfying is an understatement. Where were the fireworks, the smell of roses, and the choir of angels? What was all the hype about the bliss of sexual intercourse? Did having sex in the back seat of a car prove Bill's love? I realized sex had nothing to do with love. You could have one without the other.

I didn't hear from Bill all the next day. In the evening, I borrowed Mother's car and drove to his house. He saw the look on my face and ran from me. I chased him around the dining room table several times until his mother came out of the kitchen with a rolling pin in striking position. "You better be nice to Joan and apologize for whatever it was that got her angry. Don't give her any of your guff, she doesn't deserve it."

He ran upstairs and I followed him into his bedroom. "Joan, calm down." He grabbed me and held me tight. I began to cry. "I love you," he said.

"Well, you have a funny way of showing it. Why didn't you call me today?" Whatever he said must have worked because we continued dating until graduation.

Two months later, I wished that Aunt Grace were there to give me advice. I was in trouble. I wrote to my girlfriend at college in Arizona. "I don't know what to do. I've missed my period for two months. Help!" I placed the letter on the outgoing mail table.

The next day after school, Mother called me into her room. Peppi was by her side. "Are you pregnant?" Mother asked. Peppi handed me the letter sans the envelope.

"You opened my mail?" I shrieked.

"It was unsealed," Peppi said.

"It was not."

"It was, Joan. You probably wanted someone to find out."

I have no idea whether or not I left the envelope open. But knowing something about the psychological mind, I imagine she was right.

"Do you want to ask Bill to marry you?" Mother asked. I didn't, but I picked up the phone and called him. "Come right over," I demanded.

We went for a ride and I told him the situation. "I love you, but I'm not ready to get married," he said. I was relieved. I wasn't ready for it either. There was no need for further discussion. We drove to Johnny & Hanges, and he bought us hot dogs and fries.

Mother was happy with the decision as well. While I was out driving with Bill, she found a doctor who would take the hush money for an abortion. We drove to Manhattan where the doctor had a small operating room set up in his office and performed a D&C. I was upset about having to undergo a medical procedure, but felt no remorse about getting an abortion. Not getting one would have forced me into a situation I didn't want. I was given a prescription to prevent infection and only missed one day of school. When Jane came to get me the next morning, Mother told her that I had a bad tummy ache.

Bill and I continued dating, although my parents had forbidden me to see him.

Prom night caused a bit of a hassle as I told my parents my date was Phil Ross, a friend of Bill's, who promised to pick me up. But Phil's girlfriend forced him to rescind his offer at the last minute. We sent out word that a substitute was needed pronto. My 'prom' date rang the bell. I rushed him out of the door and down the steps. Before we reached the car, Mother, camera in hand, appeared and insisted on taking pictures of me with Phil Ross, who wasn't Phil Ross, and to this day I have no idea who he was.

I graduated in June; Bill did not. He needed to make up a class or two. I spent the summer as a counselor at a day camp. Bill and I decided it was time to date others, although we got together every so often and remain friends, even as I write this memoir.

*****

While shopping for some choice outfits on a downtown street in Paterson just before college began, I ran into a friend of my parents and my aunt's name was mentioned.

"I loved Grace," she said. "She was a beautiful person, both inside and out. So thoughtful and kind, I can't imagine why she committed suicide."

"She didn't commit suicide," I answered. "She died of pneumonia."

The woman, realizing her faux pas, quickly retracted her statement. "Oh, I'm sorry, dear, I must have gotten Grace mixed up with someone else."

"I'm sure you did!" I replied, knowing full well that her first statement must be true.

No wonder no one ever spoke about Aunt Grace's death. Was the family secret known to everyone but me?

Grace's death surely devastated me. But what if I'd been told she died; and not that she *might* die? Would I have suffered less? What if I'd been told she committed suicide, not that she died of pneumonia? Would I have struggled more?

I lost the most important person in my life the day Gracie died.

Who was there to take her place?

No one.

*****

I telephoned Peppi one day in 2007 to tell her I joined a memoir writing class.

"I'm happy to hear that. I always thought you were a better writer than an actress," she responded. I began pursuing acting in my forties (mid-life crises time), a career I dreamed about but was too frightened to attempt earlier.

"Thanks a lot." I said. This was actually a very nice compliment coming from my sister, and I had to agree. I struggled with letting myself be vulnerable on stage, so my acting "career" didn't get very far.

"I'm serious. I'm really delighted. What are you going to write about?"

"Aunt Grace, but I need to ask you a few questions." I grabbed a pen and pad.

"I don't remember much about it. What do you want to know?"

"I want to know the events surrounding Aunt Grace's death."

"No one ever discussed it with me. Dad just told me that she died while we were at camp."

"Did he tell you she committed suicide?"

"No. He told me she died of pneumonia."

"But you knew she committed suicide, didn't you?"

"Yes, of course."

"Well, who told you?"

"I don't remember just now. Can I call you back? I have to make dinner."

"I guess so," I sighed, and took three deep breaths before returning the receiver to its cradle. Peppi was no help. I tried to remember if I had a conversation with Mother about her committing suicide after my encounter with the woman on the street, but nothing came to mind. Mother had told me Gracie died before she phoned me, but left me believing it was from pneumonia.

I suppose I just became a loyal member of the "Secret Suicide Society," taking the unspoken oath to never mention Aunt Grace to family, friends, or strangers. Fortunately, Dr. Shapiro forced me to talk about it.

Peppi called me back the next morning. "A girl in my class told me it was suicide, although I can't remember how or why the subject came up."

"How old were you when she told you?" I asked.

"What year did Gracie die?"

"1950."

"I was 14 and already in high school. I think we were in chemistry class and it was October or November of that year."

"You knew back then! Why didn't you tell me?"

"It never occurred to me. Look, if you don't need me for anything else, I've got to head to the gym."

"I don't need you for anything else at the moment." The telephone clicked before I finished my sentence. It surprised me that Peppi heard about the suicide so soon after Gracie died and never mentioned it to me until now. Perhaps I was blessed by not having this information given to me then. It would have added more anguish to my overpowering guilt.

*****

When my writing of this neared completion, it occurred to me that if I was still disturbed by the loss of Gracie, what must be the consequences for Harmon and Jimmy?

I was hesitant about approaching Harmon. Years before, I sat comfortably on a Chippendale couch in his pristine living room, a glass of diet Coke atop a coaster on the coffee table. Harmon sat stiffly on a Queen Anne chair, positioned to allow for easy conversation. He held a glass of wine in his hand and listened politely as I spoke of my love for his mother and the after-effects of her death. He exhibited no emotional response to what I was telling him. At one point I began to cry, but even then he remained impassive. I excused myself to go to the bathroom, and, after exiting, saw an antique desk from Harmon's childhood. "I remember this so vividly," I exclaimed, sliding my hand across the top of this Federal Secretary desk.

Both of our homes were filled with the spoils of Mother and Gracie's lust for a good bargain. Harmon relaxed a bit as we expressed our delight in being able to continue living with such beautiful furniture. Gracie's spirit engulfed me as I looked at all the pieces I remembered seeing in her home including an American Chippendale side chair, a Windsor Captain's chair, and a scattering of Wedgewood tabletop pieces.

Harmon seemed relieved that I changed the subject and grateful when I waved goodbye. For the next few days my monologue to him and his somber expression replayed in my head like a song worm.

When I finally summoned the nerve to approach the subject again, I was scared. I put if off for several weeks. This conversation was going to involve asking for details about his mother's suicide. I wondered if he remembered anything.

When I finally called and asked, he said, "There's not a moment in my life that I don't think about that day."

I sent him the most up-to-date manuscript. He had forgotten how close I felt to Gracie and that her death caused me such pain. He admitted that talking about his mother's death caused him great distress. Reluctantly, he agreed to help, but preferred our discussions to be done by e-mail as he would need a few weeks to prepare himself to delve into the past. After not hearing from him for a month, I sent a follow up e-mail. His response was, "I'm working on it; should have something for you in a few days. It hasn't been easy." No wonder he was non-responsive that day in his living room.

On Sunday, July 23, 1950, sixteen-year-old Harmon spent the evening with his father, Don, at Yonkers Raceway watching the trotters run. They arrived home around 11:00 p.m. Harmon walked through the front door first and saw the note, which was easily visible on the desk. He read it quickly, handed it to his father, and ran upstairs.

Grace was lying on one of the twin beds in Jimmy's room, while Jimmy was asleep on the other bed. "I took her pulse while dad called for help," Harmon said. "She was still alive."

Harmon had a vague recollection of them trying to wake Grace by walking her around the room, her torso held upright by placing their hands firmly about her waist and slinging her arms around their necks.

When the ambulance was summoned, Don ordered the driver not to use a siren or flashing lights. Since it was late at night, worries over anyone seeing or hearing it were eliminated. Don and Harmon followed the ambulance to the hospital in a car. Grace was still breathing when they arrived. They stayed while the doctors pumped her stomach to empty it of sleeping pills. But the procedure weakened her. She developed pneumonia and died the following day.

As I listened to the story, I reacted the same way I did while watching a movie of the shooting of Abraham Lincoln. As the film unraveled the events leading up to his death, I kept hoping and praying for a different outcome.

The family worked diligently to keep the suicide from being made public. Don persuaded my father to use his influence with his best friend, David Cole. He was a prominent lawyer and a labor mediator who served under Franklin D. Roosevelt. Through David's sway, pneumonia became the official cause of death reported in the two local newspapers and printed on the death certificate.

Harmon never forgot the words of his mother's suicide note. *I'm at peace now. Please don't let anyone mourn me.* I knew this request was impossible, yet prayed that her first sentiment was fulfilled.

When anyone commits suicide, family members search their souls for the reason it happened and ask themselves if they could have prevented it. Did Don take blame for his wife's death? I understand he was a difficult and demanding man, although I never personally encountered that side of him. Mother brought Gracie to town to ease her depression by watching over her. Did she suffer from a sense of failure?

My gut feeling is that Lenny's death the year before was the catalyst that triggered her suicide. She was his surrogate mother when he moved into her home. In a way, Gracie lost a brother and a son, a double whammy from which she could not recover.

I wish I had asked my mother more questions about it. Yet I know that even if I had, meaningful answers wouldn't have followed. Now we can only speculate as to the reason Gracie sought death over life. Harmon said, "Her depression had to be devastating for her to leave the family, especially a five-year-old child."

*****

I continue to explore my life through psychotherapy, which brings me back to the Aunt Grace story from time to time. I'd like to write that the years in and out of analysis have wiped away all the negative effects surrounding her death, but I can't. Every time I read through the story, in order to edit my work, I cry. The tears come from a place deep inside, a place that still holds onto the roots of grief, keeping the secret of *why* it does so buried.

POSTSCRIPT

In 2016 at age 77, I was at theater watching *Finding Neverland*, a musical adaptation about a woman and her three sons who inspired J.M. Barrie to write *Peter Pan*. Peter tells the boys, "Whenever someone says they don't believe in fairies, a fairy dies." Near the end of the play, the actors reenact the scene where, in order to save Peter, Tinker Bell drinks the glass of milk in which Captain Hook put poison. Her fairy light diminishes, her voice weakens, and she barely manages to fly to Peter's shoulder to say goodbye. Peter begs the audience, "If you really, truly believe in fairies, Tinkerbell won't die. She will live if you clap your hands to let her know you believe." Before the scene starts, I recognize what is about to happen, and I burst into tears. Ridiculously deep, heartfelt sobs. The rest of the audience is clapping with delight.

My Parents' Bedroom

My parents' bedroom had wraparound windows. Sunshine engulfed me as I stepped over the threshold onto golden plush carpeting. How wonderfully unique Mother's closet was, with its full-sized window overlooking hedges separating our house from the neighbor's driveway. I spent hours sitting on the floor, imagining myself grown up, wearing one of the stunning dresses that graced her closet. My favorite was a navy sequined formal gown.

My mother, Isabelle, was as beautiful as any Hollywood actress, and the room, with its bright colors and luxurious fabrics, reflected her beauty.

I sat happily on the carved four-poster mahogany bed, covered by a white laced canopy, while Mother sat at her vanity, preparing for an evening out with my father. We chatted and laughed as I studied how she applied mascara and lipstick, and longed to wear makeup.

During afternoons when Mother was out, I played beneath billowing dust ruffles that surrounded the bed, listened to the droning sound of the vacuum cleaner rising from the floor below to let me know that our housekeeper, Lena, was close at hand.

On nights my parents went out, I watched them walk down to the car from the bedroom window, which faced the front of the house on my father's side of the room. I rarely went to that side, and I never played there. Nor did I sleep on my father's side of the bed or go into his closet. My father was as gruff as my mother was gracious, and he frightened me. Still, I made an exception on those special nights.

I loved the flair with which my mother walked. Father escorted her to the Cadillac, and opened the door. She gracefully sat down. Father made sure her gown was carefully tucked in before he closed the door, and took his place behind the wheel.

Mother smiled and waved as I watched them drive out of sight. Then I ran back to mother's side of the room to spend the night. With the help of a little foot stool, I climbed onto the tall antique bed, and turned out the light. I lay on my back, and gazed at the geometric designs on the ceiling, as lights from passing cars flashed across the window, trickled through closed venetian blinds, and made diagonal patterns across the ceiling. The cars' gentle swoosh accompanied the light, and together, they had a hypnotic effect, sending me into a deep and peaceful sleep.

During the war years, my mother's side of the room was a place of love, peace, and solace, where dreams were dreamed, and tears were shed. It was the place to go on nights I couldn't sleep. Curled up tightly between mother's warm body and the bed's edge, I felt secure. The radio constantly played as we listened to Glenn Miller, Harry James, Frank Sinatra… When news aired, it was my job to turn the radio louder because Mother's brother, Lenny, was fighting in Europe. How still we were as we listened.

I had nightmares about Hitler and was frightened of the dark. Before going to sleep, I looked under my bed to see if he was hiding there. I often dreamed that the sirens were signals that Hitler was looking through our dining room window, and we had to stay still, so he would think we were statues, not people, and leave without killing us. I also thought *enemy* and *Germany* were the same word.

My most vivid memory was V-J Day. Mother called me into her room to hear the announcement: *The war was over.* The year was 1945, and I was six years old. When the radio played the National Anthem, Mother stood me on the bed, told me to salute, and to say a prayer for the safe return of Uncle Lenny. She had tears in her eyes. When the music stopped, we hugged tightly. She picked me up, carried me downstairs, and into the kitchen, to celebrate the end of World War II with a hot fudge sundae.

Heartbreak, Tex, and Me

"My heart is broken, my heart is broken!" The front door swung open, and my older sister Peppi bounded up the stairs sobbing, "Mommy, Mommy, my heart is broken. Jerry broke my heart." I stared after her as she reached the landing and headed toward our parent's bedroom. I dared not follow. I knew better than to go anywhere near my sister when she was upset or angry. The last time I tried to get within two feet of her during one of her moods, she bopped me over the head with a phonograph record, ironically titled, "These Foolish Things Remind Me of You."

I shrugged and flung myself onto the sofa in the living room. I tried reading a comic book, but couldn't concentrate. I wondered how Jerry broke her heart. I heard of a broken arm and a broken nose, and the previous year my best friend, Jane, broke her leg when we were in third grade. The doctor put a cast on it, and she got so much attention because she had to use crutches. Everyone wanted to sign her cast. Strangers asked how it happened and offered to help with this and that. She didn't have to attend school for an entire week.

The day she came back to school, Mr. Dailey, the cutest teacher in the whole school, carried her up the stairs to class, down the stairs for recess, up again, and down again when school was over. He did this, day in and day out, until the cast was removed and placed in the corner of Jane's room as a souvenir.

I wanted more than anything in the world to break my leg. I stopped looking where I was going, leapt up and down the stairs, and ran everywhere I went. I jumped from the five-foot wall that ran the length of our backyard and bordered our property from the neighbors. All this activity only made me a better athlete.

What does a broken heart look like? How do you put it in a cast? I asked myself these questions over and over. I was sure Mother would take Peppi to the hospital or that the doctor would come shortly to mend it. I was eager to find out the answers, so I waited for something to happen. I waited, and waited, and fell asleep waiting.

"Joanie, Joanie, dinner time. Come and get it!"

I woke up with a start, not realizing I had fallen asleep, and angry that I might have missed the doctor. I rushed into the dining room and was surprised to see Peppi sitting there. She looked perfectly fine except for her long frowning face. I saw no cast, no bandages, and there was not a sign of any physical damage as far as I could see.

Everyone was quiet. No one said a word for a long time. Then Dad asked how school was that day. Peppi answered first, but she didn't say anything about her heart being broken. When it came to my turn all I could say was, "O.K., I guess."

Dinner ended in silence; the dishes were cleared, washed, dried, and put away, and still nothing was mentioned.

Later that evening, I asked Mom about it. "How did Jerry break Peppi's heart?" I whispered.

"Never mind about that! Peppi will be all right. She just needs some time to get over it. Now run along and get ready for bed." And that was that. The entire subject was dropped, and eventually forgotten—even by me.

Then one day, about a year later, I arrived home from school and hurried into the kitchen to do my after-school chore, which was to feed the cat, a stray that I had befriended several years earlier with a dish of milk. From that moment on, this kitten became a permanent member of the family. Tex was a fluffy gray cat of uncertain heritage that was quite fond of nightly rollicks through the neighborhood, and spent most of the time curled up on my pillow sound asleep. Once a year Tex would hide under my bed for a long period of time and emerge a proud mother of a litter of kittens. When it first happened we discovered, despite the cat's masculine name, which I had the privilege of giving her, that he was a she. Mother was none too pleased, and wanted to give her away then and there. She was tired of having to find homes for the kittens and hated to take them to the pound if no suitable home could be found. But after endless pleading, much hysterical sobbing, and grumbling, she allowed me to keep her. I grabbed Tex in my arms, and hugged her tightly. "You're mine," I told her. "And you're here to stay!"

But on this particular day, I was in a hurry. Jane and I were racing to see who could arrive at our meeting place first—a race I wanted to win! I opened the can of food quickly and placed Tex's dish on the floor. It was unusual for her not to be there. She always met me at the door, and didn't stop meowing until I put her bowl down. I began to call her name as I ran upstairs to change into my play clothes.

Mother's bedroom door opened abruptly. "Come in, Joanie. I have to talk with you." Mom's voice was grim. "Now!" she demanded, sensing I was about to give her an argument. Softening her voice, she added, "Sit down, Honey. I have something rather unpleasant to tell you."

I headed toward the big armchair. It was my favorite because I could comfortably curl up like a ball in it. But this time I just sat down at the edge, my feet touching the floor and my back as straight as possible. A strange sensation came over me. My heart started pounding, and I wanted to run, yet I was frozen to the spot.

"Joanie, my precious, I don't know how to tell you this. You know how Tex is always having kittens, and we have such a hard time finding homes for them?"

"Yes," I nodded.

"Well, I decided to take her to the veterinarian today to get her fixed so that she wouldn't have kittens anymore. It's a simple operation, and I was sure she would be all right. I don't know what happened, but Tex died during the operation."

My eyes filled with tears, and a sharp needle stuck through my heart. This wasn't happening. It was a big mistake. It felt like an apple was stuck in my throat, and I couldn't swallow. I pictured her cute face, and sensed her soft fur and bushy tail. The apple felt more like a grapefruit now, and the tears poured from my eyes. I couldn't speak, I couldn't move, and I found it hard to breathe.

"I'm sorry, darling. I'm really sorry."

"No, you're not," I shouted. "No, you're not. You are not sorry. You're glad. You always hated that cat, and you did it on purpose!"

I ran straight to my room and plopped on the bed. *How could mother be so mean? Tex never hurt anybody. I hate her for this. She knew how much I loved that cat. Why did she have to take her to the vet? Why didn't she tell me? Yes, why didn't she tell me? Because she knew the cat would die, that's why! She hated the cat, and she hates me! If only she hadn't done it. Oh, if only she hadn't done it. Tex would be in my room, and I could be petting her and loving her and, and . . . .* I couldn't bear the pain! I hated everything and everybody. I never wanted to see anyone again. I would stay right here in my room and never eat or sleep or play. If Tex could not be with me, then there was nothing to live for.

There was a knock at my door. "Go away," I yelled.

It was Peppi. "Jane's here, wondering why you didn't meet her."

"Go away! I don't want to see anyone. I don't want to talk to anyone. Just go away!" It seemed strange to me that, even though Janie was my best friend, and we shared everything together, that I just couldn't be with her right now. I needed to be alone. I needed to feel that queasy, painful, gripping feeling in my heart. The tears began to flow again, and my heart felt shattered into a million pieces.

I heard Peppi say, "Don't worry, Jane. Joanie just needs time to recover. She's suffering from a broken heart."

The Long Afternoon

It was early April in the innocent days of 1951 when children walking to and from school was an everyday occurrence. I was eleven, and my parents allowed me the freedom to play unattended in the streets, parks, and playgrounds of Paterson, New Jersey, an industrial town known as the "silk city" of the world.

Some days my friend Roz walked home with me instead of going in the opposite direction toward her own house; on other days, I walked home with her. One spring day we were headed to my house, when our classmates, Herbert and Harvey (who spent more time in the Principal's office than the classroom), sneaked up behind us chanting, "Rozie and Joanie sitting in a tree, F-A-R-T-I-N-G!"

The goody-two-shoes crossing guards saw us safely across the busy intersections surrounding P.S. 20 and onto the street that led to my house. Two blocks later, the boys began their torment.

"Don't you like our little song?" Herbert asked.

"We thought it was funny," said Harvey.

Roz and I tried to ignore them, not only because they were jerks and looked like Laurel and

Hardy, but because we wanted to talk about Jack. Jack was thirteen; we were almost twelve. Jack was in eighth grade; we were two years behind.

Roz had fallen off her bike doing stunts in the schoolyard, and Jack appeared with a first aid kit from his house, which happened to be right next door to the school. This handsome, blue-eyed, sandy-haired teenager applied iodine and band aids to her scraped knee.

I knew she claimed him as her boyfriend, but that didn't stop me from falling madly in love with him, too. So Jack was discussed endlessly.

All of a sudden, roly-poly Herbert skipped ahead of us and began mimicking Roz's walk.

"Get lost, you knucklehead," she said as she grabbed my hand and tried to run, but the boys blocked our path.

"Joan, your friend from the other side of the tracks is teaching you some very bad manners," Harvey teased, looking homelier, scrawnier, and more ogre-like than usual.

The boys had never acted like this before, so I figured the ragweed pollen floating in the spring air must have attacked their nostrils by the thousands, whirled around their skulls and somehow clogged up their brains, causing them to act like idiots.

"Talk to us right now, or live to regret it," Herbert demanded as he tried to stretch himself up to a dignified height.

"Not on your life! You can't scare us! Now scram!" Roz said, not stopping to consult me on the "us" part.

"Please leave us alone," I pleaded. But Herbert continued.

"Tomorrow after school we're going to hunt you down and rape you."

"What does that mean?" I asked Roz, feeling somewhat uneasy.

"You'll see what it means soon enough won't she, Harvey?" Herbert turned to his friend for approval, only to see a blank expression. Then the boys ran off laughing as we stood there, motionless, watching them disappear.

"What does rape mean?" I asked Roz when the boys were out of sight.

"I'm not sure, but I think it has something to do with taking your clothes off."

"Do you think they know what the word means?"

"I doubt it," she said, looking uncharacteristically unsure of herself.

"But what if they do know?"

Roz shrugged her shoulders. We walked in silence, then resumed our discussion as to whether or not the boys would carry out their threat. By the time we reached my house, we decided to take it seriously. One thing for sure, whatever rape was, taking your clothes off in front of boys was against the rules and something we should absolutely not do.

That afternoon we sat on the front steps of my house planning on how to avoid those two cuckoo brains the next day.

"I think we should tell my mother, don't you?" I asked Roz.

"Not on your life! She'll call my mother and then I'll be punished for starting trouble."

"But you didn't start the trouble."

"Doesn't matter, I'll get blamed anyway. I always do." We sat in silence for some time. "I have a better idea," Roz continued. "You come to my house after school."

"Wouldn't they follow us there, too?"

"Yeah, I guess," Roz mumbled. She didn't like being challenged and quickly came up with another suggestion. "Your sister could walk us home from school."

It might have been a helpful idea if her high school was closer to the grammar school, and if Peppi would be willing to help me out of a jam. Besides, she always had some kind of afterschool activity that kept her away from home until dinner.

"Well, we have to do something!" Roz said.

"I know. I know," was all I could reply. The only positive thing I could say was that maybe they were bluffing.

"Not on your life," declared Roz and came up with the master plan.

"Tell your mother you'll eat lunch at school tomorrow, and I'll tell my mother the same. We'll eat in the cafeteria and then go down to the river and stay there all afternoon until four o'clock when we can walk home safely. Be sure you let your mom know that you'll be late coming home from school."

I had never cut school before, and I wasn't sure I wanted to start now.

Roz painted a picture of the dangers we faced if the boys undressed us. "What if our clothes get ripped or torn when the boys tried to take them off? What if they decide to hide our clothes or run off with them? What would happen if our neighbors saw us running down the street in our birthday suits? How would we explain that to our parents? Talk about getting into trouble!"

I imagined our nosy neighbor, Mrs. Brawer, looking out from her giant picture window and seeing me running up the block in the nude, grabbing the phone and calling my mother. "You're right," I said, "You're right. Let's cut school."

Roz put her arm around me. "I'll take you down to the river. We'll have fun spending the afternoon, lying in the sun, eating fruit and candy. We'll sing songs and tell each other stories and talk about Jack."

How could I resist? Early that evening the wheels were set in motion. Mother agreed to my having lunch in school and said it would be all right if I stayed to play in the schoolyard. She said she'd be happy to fill my lunch box with two tuna fish sandwiches with lots of mayonnaise, an apple and a banana, chocolate chip cookies and a Clark Bar, just as I asked.

I could hardly sleep that night. I got up early, gathered my things, and rushed out the door to meet Roz before the early morning bell.

I selected one of my sandwiches for lunch to eat in the cafeteria, saving the other one for later. Then we played with our friends before taking off for our adventurous afternoon.

As each girl in line jumped into the turning rope, she sang, "Teddy Bear, Teddy Bear, turn around; Teddy Bear, Teddy Bear, touch the ground; Teddy Bear, Teddy Bear, show your shoe; Teddy Bear, Teddy Bear, please skidoo!"

We bounced a ball going through the alphabet starting with "A my name is Alice, and my husband's name is Albert, we come from Albuquerque, and we sell apples." We lifted a leg over the ball as it bounced on each letter. If we dropped the ball, our turn was over.

When the first bell rang, signaling the end of recess, we quickly headed to the Susquehanna railroad, four blocks south of school. Roz wanted to share her knowledge of all things railroad. Her home lay along a section of the tracks. She and her two older brothers played tag and hide-and-seek around the railroad yard.

As we walked arm and arm, Roz told me, "We know the Yardmaster, Benny, and he lets us tag along as he supervises the workers. He's responsible for everything that goes on, including switching inbound and outbound traffic. If I see him, I'll introduce you." We approached a field full of broken twigs, rusted nails, scraps of metal, car parts, and garbage bags with the contents spilling all over the ground. "Follow me," Roz said and ran through the field. I stood in place gathering my nerve to walk into such rubble and then moved slowly onto the field, walking very carefully, watching every step. Roz was halfway across the field when she turned around. "C'mon Spaz, move it!" she laughed. I didn't mind. Roz was fun, always coming up with exciting things to do and clever ideas on how to keep us out of trouble, like this adventurous afternoon.

That day I learned to identify all the different kinds of railroad cars: box, refrigerator, flatbed, hopper, passenger, caboose and my favorite, locomotive.

"We're going to follow the tracks to the river's edge," Roz said, leading the way. "Whatever you do, don't step, sit, walk on, or touch the third rail, or you'll get electrocuted."

"What's the third rail? I thought trains only had two rails."

"It powers the trains that run on the two rails."

Roz pointed the three rails out. The third one that lay a little off to the side looked different because it had a covering over it. At first I walked hesitantly down the center of the rails. Then it became a challenge for me to take big enough steps to get from one tie to the next, without touching down on the gravel between them. You had to add a little hop to your step if you wanted to land safely. As I became comfortable with our journey, I stopped thinking about the possibility of getting electrocuted.

When we reached the river, we climbed down the bank and made ourselves a comfortable perch by gathering dry leaves and tiny twigs into fanny-sized piles. I gobbled down my second sandwich.

Before long we realized just how cold a day in April could be. Even a sweater and jacket didn't stop us from shivering. Luckily our pockets still contained gloves and hats. We blew hot air into our hands to keep them warm.

In order to take our minds off the cold, we began to sing. *"I was dancing with my darling to the*

Tennessee Waltz when an old friend I happened to see. Introduced her to my loved one and while they were dancing my friend stole my sweetheart from me."

Then we went on. *"Detour there's a muddy road ahead detour paid no mind to what it said, Detour oh the bitter things I find should have read that detour sign."* As Patti Page was our favorite singer, we continued with "Mockin' Bird Hill," "How Much is that Doggie in the Window?" "All I Do is Dream of You," and "Old Cape Cod."

Still cold, but enjoying our concert, we switched to school safety songs like "Let the Ball Roll" and "Remember Your Name and Address." We ended our recital with Roz's rendition of "Amazing Grace," followed by my stab at "Hava Nagila."

We were sure hours had passed, but our watches told a different story. Only thirty minutes! We still had two hours to go, and we desperately needed a bathroom.

"Let's go behind these trees," Roz said and dashed away before I had a chance to veto her suggestion. I found a place that seemed quite private. Actually, the whole area was private as we were in the middle of nowhere, far from any roadways or houses. Still, I looked around to be sure no one was in view. I saw the cars passing on the far side of the river and was convinced that they could see me. I was afraid that if I squatted down some animal would come along and bite my bottom. I stood there forever, trying to gather the courage to expose myself to the cold, when I heard Roz call out, "Let's go, slow poke."

"I can't do it in the woods," I said, "and I still have to go."

Roz remembered seeing a gas station from the railroad bridge as we crossed over on the way to the river. We headed back the way we came, following our footsteps along the wooden ties of the track. We began to sing "I've Been Working on the Railroad" and didn't stop until we were in the middle of the bridge where Roz pointed out the gas station. It was very frightening looking down from the top of this high bridge, and I began to feel dizzy and a little faint. I slid down to the ground to avoid passing out and wedged myself in the tiny space that existed between the steel railing of the bridge and the railroad tracks. Roz sat down next to me and gave me a drink from her thermos.

I was beginning to feel better when we heard a loud whistle. We looked up and saw a train approaching. Roz grabbed my hand, jumped up, and ran, dragging me behind. "My lunch box!" I shouted and dropped her hand to run back.

"Are you crazy?" Roz yelled. "Run for it!" I did, trying to follow in her footsteps toward safe ground. The train was getting louder and louder. I made the mistake of looking back to see how close it was and panicked. The train was getting closer to the bridge, and I still had several feet to go before I could escape the oncoming train. My heart was pounding wildly. My feet were moving quickly, but my progress felt labored and slow like those nightmares in which you're being chased by some horrible thing and can't move no matter how hard you try. Images of me lying on a hospital bed wrapped from head to toe in bandages gave way to images of my parents weeping over my grave. At the end of the bridge my only escape was to leap from the bridge onto a steep hill. I froze. *I can't do this.* The deafening whistle of the train startled me. I looked up to see a mass of black steel almost on top of me and jumped. I landed with a thud, tumbled over, and didn't stop rolling until I reached the bottom of the slope. I was dazed and bruised and miserable.

"Wow, wasn't that exciting? We could have been killed!" Roz's voice was filled with excitement. "Are you all right?" Roz had finally noticed my terror-filled face with the tears streaming down my cheeks. She put her arms around me. "You're all right, Joan. You did well for a novice. I'm very proud of you."

I cried harder. All I wanted to do was to go home. I was dirty and tired and hurt and freezing. I'd had enough of our fun-filled afternoon, and as usual, Roz convinced me that it would not be a good idea. There would be too much explaining to do, and the punishment might be worse than the adventure. So we headed for the gas station, praying all the way that they had a restroom. Our prayers were answered. It sure felt good to be in a cozy place that had a toilet, heat, and hot water. I used the facilities, washed my hands and face, brushed off as much dirt as I could from my clothing, and combed my hair. Roz gave me her powder compact to cover the scratches on my face. I thought I looked quite presentable.

"Let's stay here till school lets out," I urged. "We still have another hour to go." Surprisingly, Roz agreed, and we sat on the floor and rested. That's when I noticed just how grimy a place this was. The walls were covered with grease and dirt, half the tiles were missing, and the only light came from a bare bulb hanging from the ceiling. I was about to suggest we leave when there came a knock on the door.

"What are you girls doing in there? You've been in there for over twenty minutes. Open up and come out!" I opened the door slowly. As I did, there was a tug from the other side of the door forcing me to lose my balance and stumble out. The door opener, dressed in a plaid hunting jacket and matching hat, gave us a skeptical look. Roz grabbed my hand and, with her nose high in the air, returned the glance with one of her own special *you know where you can go, buddy* looks.

That ended our refuge, such as it was. The problem now was where to go and what to do for the rest of the afternoon. We began walking aimlessly, weaving in and out of streets. We thought that if we strolled slowly along we could use up an hour until it was time to walk home safely.

We did fairly well, but not well enough. Two-thirty. Still another half hour to go, and we were only three blocks from school.

"What should we do now?" I asked Roz.

"Let's sneak into the school!"

"Are you crazy?" It was my turn to ask the same rhetorical question.

"I have to go to the bathroom."

"Why didn't you go at the gas station?"

"Because I didn't have to!" she snapped.

It was a stupid idea to go into the very building we were desperately avoiding so that Herbert and Harvey wouldn't take off our clothes, and where, in fact, we should have been all afternoon, and where I wished we had been all afternoon. Yet, once again I followed Roz's lead.

The school was divided into two sections. Kindergarten through fifth grade was housed in the old building while grades six through eight were in the new extension. As sixth graders, we should have used the bathroom in the new building, but it was easier for us to sneak into the old building because there were no goody-two-shoes monitors stationed in the halls. Luck was with us. We managed to get into the girl's room without being noticed.

But our luck did not hold. An unfamiliar teacher walked in and questioned us as to why we were there. I stood frozen, my mind a blank, as Roz fabricated a reason for us being there. Whatever she said worked, and we promised to go right back to class and hurried out the door. The next thing I knew we were huddled beneath the stairwell and squeezed into the far corner. We spent the rest of the time in that position hoping no one would see us.

It seemed an eternity until the last bell rang and the hallways filled up with the noisy sounds of children as they filed out of the doors. Mingling with the masses of other kids, and with our heads bowed, we sneaked out of the building as easily as we sneaked in. It was almost over. All we had to do was get home safely and our misadventure would end.

We hid behind the corner candy store until we saw our 6th grade class leave the building. We watched Harvey and Herbert run out the door, punching each other in the arm as they skipped down the stairs and headed toward the crossing guards. I wanted Roz to walk home with me, and she wanted me to walk home with her. I was tempted, but I ached all over and the call of a hot bubble bath was stronger. This time I did not give in; neither did Roz. So we agreed to go our separate ways and to call each other if and when we arrived home safely.

Once alone, I was sure I had made a mistake. Most of the kids had already scattered and were half way home by the time I got started. I felt secure enough for the first two blocks where the crossing guards were still on duty. But after that, the streets were deserted and there was no one to protect me. I was sure the boys were waiting for me behind every tree and bush. My heart was pounding, and my eyes were searching the landscape every inch of the way. What a relief to see my house come into view—one block more to go. I quickened my pace, broke into a run, and landed at my front door, huffing and puffing.

I collapsed on the living room floor and let forth a deep and appreciative sigh. Home never felt better. The phone rang. It was Roz. She had made it home without incident. How about that, I thought, with a mixture of relief and disappointment. After all we endured trying to avoid the boys' threat of rape; I still didn't know what the word meant.

Work and the Jewish American Princess

Synonyms for work are job, occupation, calling, trade, profession, task and employment. Each of these words has a slightly different impact on my senses.

Job – While growing up as the daughter of a wealthy family in the forties and fifties, it never occurred to me that I would ever need to find a job. I was groomed to be a wife and mother. My career was to find an eligible husband. It was the only career in which I found dubious success. Most women of my ilk only sought work if they did not find a mate in college. Fewer women, and, as I now see, wiser women, found a husband *and* a career.

The job market for women seemed limited to teacher or nurse; neither appealed to me. In my first year of college, I eloped. Twelve months later I had a baby; two years more and I had a divorce, which temporarily ended my career as wife and homemaker.

Being without a single skill or qualification, I enrolled in secretarial school. Upon graduation, I got a job with a small company which went out of business within my first year. It was just as well. I had married my second husband, who encouraged me to brave a new job as a secretary. Within months of being hired, I was forced to quit due to a bad case of pregnancy.

It wasn't until I was 35 that I got a real job with Western World Insurance Company, complete with benefits, periodic raises, and a chance for advancement. I advanced from a clerical position to a junior underwriter. I did very well and enjoyed the experience. I was next in line for a senior underwriting position when I quit. I lacked the confidence to assume this type of responsibility and was sure that I would not live up to the expectations of the department head. This fear was so crippling, I lied to my boss, saying, "My father wants me to work with him in his real estate business." Not to feel myself totally dishonest, I looked for work in the field, and was hired by Helmsley Spear to rent commercial space.

But history repeats itself. I was fairly successful in my first year of sales but hated the pressure and anxiety it caused me. During my working hours of 9-5, the obligation of making cold calls without much success weakened my endurance. If I took a day off, I felt guilty for wasting time. I couldn't handle the world of cutthroat competition. I was a novice in the field and needed help, but fellow brokers were not apt to give advice. I quit. That was my last attempt to hold down a permanent job.

All was not lost by the experience though. Years later, I used my cold calling experience to sell myself at auditions.

Occupation – One of the definitions in Webster's New Collegiate Dictionary for the word occupation is *the principal business of one's life*. I must admit that the process of discovering who I am, and what animates me is, in fact, the principal occupation of my life.

Through the help of numerous psychiatrists and psychologists, teachers and educators, spiritual leaders and mystics, I have been on a path of self-discovery, which is difficult and rewarding. Without such a path, I may never have been able to write this essay. Nor would I have the understanding that I'm my own judge, critic, and motivator. My occupation is limitless, and I shall never have to retire from it.

Calling – All of my life I have wanted to be an actress. It wasn't the glamour and glitz that Hollywood offered; it was a deep-rooted need to be someone else, anyone else, as long as it wasn't me. As an actress I could portray another's life, live in their world, and be absent from my own.

As I diligently worked at my *occupation*, I came to like myself more and more, and the *calling* to be an actress never ceased. By mid-life, with the help of a therapist, I gathered enough ego strength and courage to pursue an acting career. Unfortunately, after all the years devoted to left-brained thinking, bogged down with cognitive skills, I had lost my creativity and imagination. Developing my right-brain skills—to become emotional, intuitive, and vulnerable on stage—was a struggle.

I worked to bring these two antagonistic spheres into harmony, hoping to accomplish my childhood dream to be a good actress. That goal came to fruition years later in an acting class performance at the 92Y. I had been going to auditions from the time we moved into Manhattan in 1987, and eventually signed up with a company called ArtGroup that would take me. It was Community Theater within the stage performance capital of the world. Although I'd taken many acting classes, this group gave me experience, in acting, as well as directing. My biggest obstacle was allowing myself to be real on stage. During rehearsal, I often heard the director shout, "Stop acting, Joan." I continued to audition outside of ArtGroup until 2008 when my husband and I decided to update our kitchen. We needed to stay elsewhere during that time, and I never returned to auditioning.

It was 2009 when I joined the 92Y, and took the acting class with Scott Klavan. We worked on monologues, and I was determined to find that vulnerability I lacked. Perhaps it was the break I took from the theater, my maturity, or that the lack of pressure, but I was able to get to that magnificent place where I actually became the character I was portraying. I not only felt it, but it was verified by several audience members.

Trade – In order to have a trade, one needs manual or mechanical skills. Shoe makers, auto mechanics, carpenters and plumbers are tradesmen. These people work with their hands as well as their heads.

Within *our* affluent Jewish community, one was taught to value the ability to use one's head, not one's hands. Higher education was the goal. One got ahead through knowledge. Parents sacrificed the good life in order to put their sons through college. Having a trade was not a worthy aspiration. The closest I got to a trade was the shorthand and typing I learned in secretarial school.

Profession – Now that's more like it! It's good for a nice Jewish boy to become a lawyer; better yet, he should become a doctor. Accountants were also acceptable. For this I am most grateful, as my third and final husband was a successful Certified Public Accountant.

Every mother wanted her daughter to marry a professional man. Having a profession guaranteed success. Success was based on how much money you had. Being a loving spouse and father were secondary to making money. The important things in life were being able to afford a maid, belong to a country club, have a different dress for each major social occasion, and send your children to the best camps.

It never occurred to me to become a professional woman. I didn't believe I had the intelligence and ability to do so. It took years before I stopped thinking of professionals in terms of a male-dominated world, and more years before I felt comfortable placing my trust in a female doctor or lawyer—although I was happy to know they existed. Now my lawyer, broker, and doctors are all female. *We've come a long way, baby!*

Task – My life is filled with tasks. I create them. My husband called me "The Project Queen." There is nothing I hate worse than waking up in the morning without plans. I will clean the house if necessary. Between my other obligations and pastimes, I am grateful for tasks. They sometimes accumulate when I become busy with bridge, acting, writing, and vacationing, but they are always there waiting for my return: reading and erasing my e-mails, filing papers, shopping for clothes, studying bridge, rehearsing my monologues, and organizing anything and everything that needs organization.

When upset, I take out my aggression on menial tasks like cleaning out the refrigerator and mending and sorting my socks. When unhappy, tasks act as a bridge to a happier state of mind. Is it possible that God created tasks to keep us out of trouble and away from loneliness?

Employment – definition: an activity in which one engages or is employed. According to that definition, I engage in tasks which bring me happiness and well-being. I believe that one shouldn't think in terms of acquired wealth in choosing employment, but to be solely driven by a calling, if one is lucky to have one, and can afford to follow their dream. Eric Morris once told me I'd never be successful as an actress because I wasn't hungry enough. When I spoke with Eric to get his permission to write about him, he was surprised he said that to me and expressed regret.

Out of necessity, people must devote more time to their employment because the bills must be paid, and less time to their personal life.

If this employment is not spent fairly harmoniously and with relative joy, how can one expect to find happiness in one's personal life?

I'm fortunate to have my personal life as my employment; I'm continually engaged with one interest or another. My livelihood does not depend on my employment. It has been said that this is a curse as well as a blessing. The blessing is that I am able to pursue happiness and self-fulfillment without the thought of monetary needs. The curse is that this same freedom has prevented me from sticking with a chosen field of interest long enough to succeed at it. Would I have made a good underwriter or real estate salesperson if I had been forced to stay on the job because I needed the money? Would waiting on tables have aided me in becoming a successful actress because success would have meant financial security?

It's possible that my life might have been very different had I been born into a less well-to-do family. Still, I am what I am. My life experiences are my realities.

The battle is not lost. I continue to be employed by life itself, and my occupation of self-improvement continues. It is conceivable that one day I will finish the race feeling successful, even without having been fruitful in the business world.

Till then, it is my belief, and one I pass on to my children and grandchildren, that the significance of work, whether it be through a job, occupation, calling, trade, profession, task or employment, is to strive toward greater growth and understanding and to enjoy the journey.

"Dirty" Paper and Other Salvagings

"Where's the paper?" my husband asked.

"We don't get a paper," I said.

"Not a newspaper, the copy paper!"

"It's right next to the printer."

"That's dirty paper."

"It isn't dirty; the other side is perfectly clean."

"I need to print the tax return."

"Is it the final tax return to be put in an envelope and mailed to the IRS?"

"No."

"We are not wasting good paper on practice sheets."

And so it went every year since we downloaded Turbo Tax onto our computer, and I became aware of my husband's paper consumption because I sat by his side feeding the program the required data, and pressing *print* when requested.

*****

"You hardly touched your dinner plate," I said to my son.

"I wasn't very hungry," he answered.

"Then why did you add soup and an appetizer to your order if you knew you weren't very hungry?"

"I'll finish it tomorrow for lunch."

And so it went whenever I treated my children and, in later years my grandchildren, to dinner and they didn't finish what they ordered. My son and his wife were the worst offenders. Always over ordering, and then making a pretense of taking the leftovers home to have for lunch the next day. My grandchildren tattled on their parents that the doggie bag was put into the refrigerator until the food rotted, and then it was thrown out. From then on, I began to restrict their overindulgences by asking beforehand how hungry they were, what they planned to order, and suggesting that wastefulness is probably one of the seven deadly sins.

Where most people discard a tube of toothpaste when nothing comes out after the first squeeze, I cut the tube in half, stick my brush in, and extract enough goop to repeat the process every day for weeks, if I remember to secure the two halves together after each use. Bottles are no exception to the *no waste* rule. They get turned upside down, and as the slogan for Maxwell House coffee goes, the contents were good to the last drop.

I came into a world of rationing during WW2, and by the time I was six, was well schooled in the art of frugality. I was taught not to waste anything.

As the family sat down for dinner, Mother reminded me to eat everything on my plate because there were starving children in Europe. When I left a room, Father barked, "Turn off the lights, we don't waste electricity." The fun part was saving the foil from our gum wrappers and turning them into giant balls, and collecting pennies in a jar to send to the government because they needed the silver, zinc and copper for the war effort. Mother helped by giving me used aluminum foil from the kitchen, and handing me pennies from her purse each night.

For as long as I can remember, my father's response to non-essential purchases, like chachkies, was, "What the hell do you need that for?" He never spent money on personal items for himself; clothes were of no interest to him, and mother had to drag him to the store when necessity forced him to buy something new. His factory office was furnished with old heavy furniture from days gone by, while his brother-in-law partner had a designer office with all the latest décor.

Father was generous to his family, freely spending money on restaurants, entertainment, travel and membership in an exclusive country club. He set up trust funds for his children, supported his father and stepmother, and loaned his sister money to start a business, which later became a multimillion dollar venture.

My mother was more lavish in her willingness to spend Father's money. She bought expensive clothes, jewelry, and antiques. Both parents were thriftier when it came to their children. I remember her reluctance to buy me a Girl Scout uniform because it would be a waste of money if I quit. To put this expenditure into perspective, when my daughter became a girl scout in 1970, the entire outfit cost me thirteen dollars. How much could it have been in 1946? As a teenager, I fell in love with a reversible pleated plaid skirt in a downtown department store where we had a charge account, and got reprimanded for buying it without her permission. I was sure Mother scolded me because she didn't like the skirt. I never bought anything on my own again while my mother was around to help me.

There was no denying that I took after my father's monetary values. While living in New Jersey, I pinched pennies wherever I could although I wasn't a big coupon user, or comparison shopper. My father was on my shoulder whispering *What the hell do you need that for?* whenever I shopped for myself. I had no problem spending freely where he spent freely.

Once I moved to Manhattan, it became impossible to remain thrifty. I didn't take taxis; I'd subway it or walk. I based my tip on the cost of the food only, without the tax, and I never over tipped. To save money, I food shopped on days when I had to drive to New Jersey. One day coming home from a New Jersey shopping trip, I saw the refrigerator filled with groceries. "Where did these come from?" I asked my husband.

"The Food Emporium," he replied.

"I've been trying to save money shopping in New Jersey, and you went to Food Emporium?"

"Yep! I never said you had to shop in New Jersey."

What the hell am I doing? I thought. I realized that I had two choices: I could hold onto my parsimonious ways, go completely berserk, and wind up in the nut house, or I could give up this insane obsession of waste not want not, and lead a normal life, which is the choice I made for the most part. The transition happened slowly. I stopped food shopping in New Jersey, and I pushed my father from my shoulder whenever I went shopping for myself.

Wasteful behavior still haunts me. It's pervasive in our society and culture, but I no longer go whacky over it. I'm happy to report that my grandchildren saw the wisdom of not over ordering or overspending, and adhere to the value of saving for a rainy day.

However, I still get the most out of tubes and bottles, and I still use dirty paper.

How I Met My First Husband
(A Monologue)

How did I meet your grandpa? Well, it all started on the closing night of the premiere performances of "Blue Men on Mars." The year was 1958. Along with four other new thespians of the drama club, our debut performance consisted of standing across the back of the stage, donning blue make up, for two and a half hours without saying a word. Still it was a thrill just to be on stage.

Now, the cast party was held at Tully's Tavern, where the cast and crew mingled and drank with the locals. Earl, the Director, kept the atmosphere lively and everyone happy by constantly feeding the juke box with quarters.

Then the star of the show arrived at the old watering hole, fashionably late, to bless us with her presence, and we dutifully gave her thunderous applause. Oh my Lord, you'd think she was a famous actress, instead of a snot-nosed senior at Upsala College in East Orange, New Jersey. That's where I was a freshman.

Twice I was asked to dance. Once by a tipsy townie, who seemed to know his way around the joint, and slurred his words so badly that my side of the conversation consisted of only one word, "What?"

My other dancing partner was a twenty-year-old, brown-haired, hazel-eyed, Roman-nosed friend of Earl. His 6'6" height fascinated me, along with his worldly wise sophistication. I had no idea what to say to him. I put my head on his chest and said something stupid about the joys of dancing with someone much taller than myself.

A few days later, I was summoned to the first floor of our dorm to receive a phone call. I ran down three flights of stairs. Gertrude shoved the receiver toward me as if it were a dirty-diapered baby.

"Who is it?" I asked.

"Some guy you met Saturday night." She slammed the phone into my hand and hurried back to the study room to finish her homework, catch up on her reading, and listen to her classical music.

Oh my God, I hope it's not that Tipsy Townie. "Hello."

"Hi, this is Marty. I met you at the cast party, and Earl gave me your number."

Thank God, not the Townie. Wait a minute; wait a minute, what if Mr. Tipsy is also a friend of Earl?

"I met so many people Saturday night. I'm not sure I can place you by your voice."

"We danced together." He sounded a bit perturbed.

"I was dancing with strangers all night," I exaggerated. "Which one were you?"

"The tall one. You put your head on my chest."

Yippee, the tall one! "Ah yes, I remember you very well. You're Earl's friend." Then using my best theatrical lilt, I added, "He's such a dear!"

"Yes, he is."

"How do you know each other?"

"We met in North Carolina doing summer stock."

"Summer stock! Oh, that is so exciting."

We chatted a little longer about summer stock, about his friendship with Earl, about the drama club, about where we grew up – he in Flushing, Queens, me in Paterson, NJ. Finally, he asked me out on a date, by the end of which, I was head over heels in love. Why not? He was tall. He was handsome. He could dance. He sang "Mr. Froggie Went A' Courting," a song I never heard before. Most amazingly, though, he liked me. He liked *me*! What more could a 17-year-old girl want? Four months later, your grandfather and I eloped.

What? No, no, that's a different story for another time.

Big Al and My New Dress

My first job, after graduating secretarial school in 1962, was at the Plunkett Chemical Company. I was interviewed and hired by Dori, the office manager. We became fast friends, both having graduated from the same high school two years apart, both divorced, and in our early twenties.

On a Friday, three months after I was hired, Dori asked me to meet her in the ladies room. "I'm freaked out. Nick wants me to come to Newark tomorrow to see him. I don't want to go alone."

I held Dori close to stop the shaking. I had no idea who Nick was. "I'll go with you," I said.

The next day on our drive to Newark, Dori filled me in on the details behind her anxiety.

"I was seventeen when Ralph and I met and fell in love. He was twenty-one, and fresh out of the army. Six months later, he introduced me to his parents. As we were sitting in their living room chatting, fourteen-year-old Nick came in the front door. Without as much as a hello, their mother yelled out, *Did you cut school again?*

No, Mom, Nick replied.

The mother shook her head, and said, *Come here Loser. Meet your brother's fiancée before you run out to see your hoodlum friends.*

Leave the boy alone, Nick's father said, as he patted him on the back. *He's doing the best he can; isn't that right son?*

My ass, he's doing his best. He's a worthless punk, the mother said, and stormed into the kitchen.

Thanks anyway, Dad, Nick said, lowering his head. With wet eyes, he left the house and slammed the door. His father started after him, placed his hand on the doorknob, paused, turned, and headed for the kitchen. I asked Ralph what that was all about.

Ralph lit a cigarette and said, *That's the reason I joined the army at seventeen. I got tired of my mother's negativity and my father's inability to set things right.*

I vowed never to go back to that house. Yet when Ralph asked me to drop off a package, I acquiesced. Nick answered the door. *Is your Mother home?* I asked.

Nick said, *Not at the moment, I'm happy to say.*

I told him I had a package for his mother. Nick opened the door wide, pointed to a table standing next to the kitchen door, and said, *You're welcome to leave it on the table over there.* I followed his directions, thanked him, and turned to leave. *I was just going to have a beer. Please join me. I've been alone all day,* he pleaded. I heard his yearning, and observed his woeful countenance. I understood his pain, seeing their mother's negativity flair up in Ralph's behavior. I knew Nick sensed my compassion, and agreed to come in, but declined the beer.

Nick dropped onto the couch and stretched out his legs. *No one can ever do anything right in Mom's eyes, least of all me. I kept trying to please her, but now I just do what I want.*

I asked him what it is he wanted, and wondered if this was the first time anyone took an interest in his life. *Shit, I don't know. I'm having fun, driving around town, and taking my friends for a ride.*

I reminded him that he didn't have a license yet. *Nah. I steal a car, drive it around and park it in the neighborhood so it can be found. No harm done, right?*

That could get you into trouble, I said. *You know you're breaking laws, don't you?* I said this with caring concern, without judgment in my voice. We talked for over an hour. By the time I left, Nick's eyes had come alive and he was smiling.

From then on, during my courtship with Ralph, Nick appeared out of nowhere and interfered with our privacy. He'd monopolize my attention, which was easy to do. Ralph would slip him a five dollar bill. *Go get yourself a beer, kid, Dori's my girl,* he'd say. Ralph ran out of fives before Nick ran out of fascination with me.

A year later, a week before Ralph and I took our vows, Nick was caught stealing a car and sentenced to the juvenile detention center. He finished high school there before he was released. Not wanting to go home, he asked Ralph if he could stay with us until he got settled. Surprisingly, Ralph agreed, but became increasingly jealous of my relationship with Nick. We were so at ease with one another, and Nick was showing signs of changing for the better. One night, Ralph came home drunk, and kicked Nick out."

"Was Nick the cause of your breakup?" I asked.

"No, Ralph's drinking and inability to keep a job finally got to me. After hearing Nick's stories about their mother, I realized that Ralph's problems were deeper than I had thought. His drinking increased and he lost his job. When I couldn't handle it any more, I left."

"Did you ever see Nick again?"

"He called me at work. I was very attracted to him and knew that he was in love with me . . . but he was still my brother-in-law for goodness' sakes! I told him that he must stop calling me. Convinced that I meant what I said, he moved to Newark where his life went from bad to worse. He continued stealing cars, wound up in jail, and I haven't had contact with him since he was incarcerated."

*****

When we reached Newark, we drove, seemingly in circles, until we reached the number and street written on a torn piece of paper. Dori found a parking space in front of an empty lot, strewn with auto parts, garbage and refuse one associates with a hospital.

"Do you think it's safe to park here?" I asked.

"Probably not, but at least it's only a few houses down from this address." The houses on the block were identical two story structures lined up side by side with five steps leading up to a porch. When new, these homes were surely beautiful. Now, they were chipped and faded, porches sagged, the steps worn and many windows were cardboard covered. Dori led the way up the stairs and knocked firmly on the door – the bell was out of order. A broad-shouldered man in his late twenties and six feet tall, with dark black hair and sharp Dick Tracy features, answered the door.

"Hi," Dori said. "I'm looking for Nick."

"You must be Dori. Come on in." His voice was scratchy and deep, his smile inviting.

"Will our car be all right in front of that empty lot?" I asked, pointing down the street.

He laughed. "You ladies will be just fine. We've got friends." He stepped aside as we entered the house. He put his arm around my waist, smiled at me, introduced himself as Big Al and guided us into the living room where we met JJ, a middle aged honcho who greeted us with a finger crushing handshake. He wore a black double breasted suit with a burgundy shirt. His nails were polished as well as his shoes. He stood a bit too close for comfort and his gaze undressed us as his lips pulled back into a lewd smile.

Little Louie, a skinny teenaged kid wearing khaki pants and a T-shirt, nodded hello from the corner of the room. He held a phone in one hand and wrote notes on a pad with the other.

Nick, in an apron and a baseball cap, burst into the room from the kitchen, embraced Dori in a bear hug, and didn't let go. "I can't breathe," Dori said, and Nick released his grip. Facing away from his friends, Nick wiped his eyes with the back of his hand before turning to me.

"So, you're Joan. Dori told me all about you on the phone." He put his arm around my shoulder and gave it a friendly squeeze. Nick was handsome – no, he was gorgeous – bright blue eyes, a dazzling smile, and long brown hair that hung over his brow. I had to restrain myself from running my fingers through it and flipping it out of his eyes.

"Now, if you folks will excuse us, we'll head upstairs for a private talk," he said as hand in hand he led Dori out of the room leaving me alone with three strange men. *What do I do now? Better turn on the charm. Drop those tense shoulders Joan, and whistle a happy tune.* "Can I get you a cup of coffee?" Big Al asked, bringing me out of thought.

"Sure, thanks. That would be nice," I said a little too loud.

"Sit down, Joanie, make yourself at home." *Joanie?* He gestured toward the sofa which was covered in a lush damask fabric. For the first time I saw the fine furnishings which were incongruous with the surrounding neighborhood.

The phone rang non-stop. I smiled at JJ and Little Louie. "You guys sure are popular," I said, and took a seat.

JJ sat next to me on the couch and asked, "Where ya from?"

"Hackensack." I shifted my weight, leaning closer to the side arm of the couch.

"Ya married?"

Luckily Big Al came in with a tray of coffee and cookies. "Try one," he said, placing the tray on the table in front of the couch. "Nicky just made them. That kid sure knows how to bake."

"More than just cookies, right Al?" JJ said, and laughed, delighted with his own humor.

Al squeezed in between JJ and me; I immediately relaxed. In spite of Al's rough exterior, he exuded warmth that comforted me in this uncomfortable situation.

"Get Nick, we've got to go," Little Louie said, finally hanging up the receiver. "We've got to go to Tony's."

Before long Dori and I were squeezed into the back seat of Big Al's car. Nick was sitting shotgun. We were on our way to Tony's Bar and Grill, a local hangout with a rustic motif, and sawdust on the floor. We were seated in the last booth farthest from the door and told to order whatever we wanted. The boys disappeared into a room behind the bar.

"It's your lucky day, baby doll," Nick said to Dori fifteen minutes later. "Are you ready to receive a new wardrobe?"

"What are you talking about?" Dori asked.

"Some dresses fell off a truck, and Harry is bringing a bunch over for you - size 12, right?"

"They actually fell off of a truck? How did that happen?" I asked. Dori kicked me under the table. "What?"

My question went unanswered until Dori and I were in the ladies room trying on the clothes. I slipped into a blue and white dress. "I can't accept one of these. I'd feel too guilty."

"Don't be ridiculous," Dori said. "You'd be a fool not to take that one. It looks dynamite on you." It was my first and last experience with stolen goods. To this day I won't even buy pirated pocketbooks on the street.

"Huba, huba," Big Al said, as he admired my new outfit. "Let's take the girls to Delmonico's for a steak dinner tonight. They can show off their new get-ups."

JJ ordered for the table: wine, salad, shrimp, steak, fries, creamed spinach, dessert and coffee. Expense didn't seem to be an issue. Left-over food didn't seem to faze them. It was fun being with a group of people who didn't worry about such things, and treated us like queens.

When we arrived home, JJ and Little Louie went straight into the house. Al pulled up to Dori's car and she and Nick got out. Al and I chatted awhile in the warmth of his car.

"I'd like to see you again." Al said. "Can I have your telephone number?" My heart began to race. I liked Al. He was nice, and I enjoyed being treated so elegantly, but I didn't want to date him.

"Why don't I come back with Dori every time she comes to see Nick?"

"All right," Al said. I saw the disappointment in his face. I was relieved to see he was a gentleman.

On our drive home, Dori said, "I'm not planning on seeing Nick again. I just said I'd be in touch soon." I was glad that I didn't have to break my promise to Big Al.

A few weeks after our trip to Newark, the local papers had an article about a gangland killing in Newark. A low level Mafia thug was found dead behind the wheel of his car with three bullets in his head. That thug was Big Al.

Three months after Big Al met his end, Dori became engaged to be married, and phoned Nick. "I just called to let you know I'm remarrying," she told Nick after a brief conversation. There was a long pause.

"I guess I should congratulate you," he said in a monotone voice.

"That would be nice, Nick. After all, I know you want me to be happy just as I want what's best for you."

"Who's the lucky man?"

"His name is Mark. He's very loving."

After another long pause, Nick asked, "When's the big day?"

Dori told him the date, but not the time or the place. On the day of her wedding, Nick attempted a botched robbery, and shot a policeman to death. The story was in all the papers with day long broadcasts on the radio and TV.

I never wore the dress again.

Postscript

Nick was given a life sentence. He redeemed himself by becoming one of the founders of "Scared Straight," a program dedicated to turning hoodlum teens away from crime, and out of jail.

Ah, to Be an Actor!

I wait in the green room for the stage manager to give the half hour call. *I better check the script before I go on.* It's my habit to review lines before each performance. But my script is not lying next to me. I look for it in the dressing room, on the stage, behind the stage, in the orchestra. I can't find it anywhere.

I approach other actors and ask if I can borrow their script. Most say they didn't bring one to the theater. Some glare at me because I'm interfering with their warm up. A few are talking on their cell phones and turn away.

I retrieve a script from under a table and try to find my lines. Several passages are marked with a yellow highlighter which keeps me from catching sight of my lines. I can't focus. The type is blurred; the words are impossible to read.

I turn to the cover on the script. It's missing. I can't remember the name of the play we're doing. I walk into the dressing room and ask the ingénue who is primping at the mirror what it is. She shrugs. I find the director and ask, "What play are we doing? I don't know any of my lines. I don't remember rehearsing this play!" He laughs at me, shakes his head, and walks away.

I hear the stage manager call, "Places everyone."

I stand in the wings and look at the script one last time for something familiar: a line, a cue, an entrance, an exit. I panic. What am I going to do? I'm pushed onto the stage, "That's your cue, babe!" My body jerks and twitches. I feel the urge to pee. I wake up with clenched teeth and a pounding heart. Consciousness never felt so good.

1972

We were on the beach, stretched out on a blanket borrowed from the motel rooms and gazing at the stars and the moon. It was not quite at its fullest, maybe three quarters I thought, and wished I remembered my fractions well enough to play around with the percentages.

"Are you really a waiter at the Auto Pub?" I asked. I sat up to hear the answer, extended my legs and stretched over to touch my toes.

"Why do you ask? Would you not fall in love with a waiter?" Stanley replied, rolling over on his side to face me.

"I'm sure I could fall in love with a waiter, but I wouldn't marry one." I took a handful of sand and let it slip through my fingers.

We were on our second date. Our respective children were on the third floor of the Sun & Surf Inn; females in one room, males in the other. The kids were watching television. At least that's what we hoped.

It was the day before Yom Kippur 1972, and we had decided to spend that hot September weekend on the beach with the kids. Stan wanted to go to Robert Moses State Park, being a resident of

Long Island, but I wanted to go to the Jersey Shore, being a native of that state. I won.

*****

The above event wouldn't have happened without a phone call I received the previous June, a call that changed the direction of my life. Barbara, my closest childhood friend, moved to the east coast of Florida several years prior and reported being happier there than she had ever been living in New Jersey. I wanted to be happy, too. So I applied to several colleges in this warm and joyous climate to further my education and get away from the wintery frosts of the northeast, as well as from my two icy ex-husbands. I was in my fifth year of divorce from husband number two, and I desperately needed a change. I stopped folding the laundry and picked up the phone.

"What's new and depressing?" I heard at the other end. It was John. I met John between my second and third marriages at a New Hampshire singles resort called Lake Tarleton. John was single. I was told that men who have never been married don't like dating divorced women with children. So when John asked me who I lived with, I said, "My family," knowing he'd think I was referring to my parents. "Do you work?" he asked. "Yes, for my father," I replied, leading him to believe I was single.

Although he was shocked when two children appeared at the door the night he picked me up for our first date, we continued dating for some time. Upon my request, he arranged for us to see Jack Jones, a singer I adored, who was appearing at a costly night club in Manhattan. When we broke up the following week, he proclaimed, "We may not have gone out in a blaze of passion, but we sure went out in a blaze of expense."

John always began his conversations with that same question. "What's new and depressing?" He was a lawyer – he loved questions. He then asked, "Are you dating anyone?

"No. You cured me of wanting to ever date again." He laughed.

"Well, the reason I'm calling is because I gave your number to someone I met at a party the other night and he's going to call you *tomorrow*. I wanted to give you a heads up."

"What's his name?" I asked.

"Stanley Faust."

I made the mistake of joking, "You mean like the devil?" That gave John the license to relay the story of Faust in great detail and then make a point of telling me that Faust was the name of the man who made a pact with the devil and not the devil himself. I already knew that, but I let it slide. It was more than enough time to say goodbye and hang up the phone.

I didn't hear from Stanley the next day, or anytime during that month of June, nor did July or August produce such a phone call. By Labor Day, I had all but forgotten John's phone call, and my plans for moving to Florida were in full swing.

Then the day after Labor Day, on the evening on the 5th of September, lo and behold, the phantom Stanley placed his call.

*****

I was already packed and waiting by the window for our trip to the seashore by 9:00 a.m. Stanley and his three children pulled into my driveway at 10:00. I ran to open the door in greeting. Eleven-year-old Lori, the most curious of the three, jumped out of the car first and ran past me with the excuse of needing the bathroom. But I spotted her eyes checking out the furnishings as she found her way to the john. David, the oldest, swaggered out of the car, Fonzie style, greeting me with a "Heeeeeey" as he slid past me at the doorway, making sure his body didn't get anywhere near mine. Six-year-old Robert, his thick brown hair falling over his forehead and ears, met me with the trusting innocence of childhood. Stanley, grinning like the proud Papa he was, walked up behind his brood and kissed me on the cheek. "Are you ready to hit the road?" he asked. Not waiting for a reply, he ordered his kids to use the bathroom before we left.

I introduced my son, Michael, a self-conscious boy of thirteen, and called his attention to the fact that he and David were the same age. I summoned Jenny to join the group, and she slowly descended the staircase and uttered a timid "hello" in the softest of tones. At eight, she hadn't yet outgrown her bashful ways when confronted with new situations.

Michael, being the tallest of the group, was placed in the front seat between Stanley and me, while the other four struggled to find comfort in the back seat. Our drive down to Point Pleasant began peacefully, but soon, as we progressed down the Garden State Parkway, the children were chatting away about their individual fun-filled adventures.

We were beginning to smell the salt ocean air when Michael, for no apparent reason (except perhaps to enter the conversation) said; "My father is 6'6" tall." Jenny immediately offered that her father was 5'9" tall, which caused some confusion to the Faust children.

"That doesn't make any sense," David said.

"Your father can't be 6'6" and 5'9" at the same time," Lori insisted.

A lively discussion followed until it was all straightened out. Fortunately, I had told Stanley about my previous marriages and births on our first date; otherwise, he might have lost control of the car, and, instead of plunging into the briny ocean, propelled us headfirst into a deep and dark abyss.

*****

I was propped up in bed surrounded by four fluffy pillows, my Psych book opened to chapter 1. I read each chapter a minimum of three times, so the knowledge would somehow stick to my brain. I was never a high-quality student.

I thought back to my parent's trip to Europe. Aunt Sonny came to care for me while they traveled. How I balked the first night she insisted on helping me with homework. I had a list of words to study for a fifth grade spelling test.

"I already studied them," I said.

"That's good! Let me see the word list," she said. I rummaged through my book bag, which hadn't been opened since I returned from school and held out a crumpled sheet of paper. She sat down with a doubtful look. "If you spell them correctly, you can watch television." She proceeded to quiz me. I failed miserably. "I want you to write each word on your forehead with your finger," she smiled. "It will imprint the word on your brain so you'll remember how to spell it."

She was right. The next day I got 100 on my test. Every night after that, I helped her clear the table and wash the dishes. I set my spelling words on the table, and sat down, ready to study. When my parents returned, I begged Mother to help me with homework, but she never did. My grades declined until, once again, travelling whisked my parents away and Aunt Sonny came back.

Now that I had matured into a college student, it appeared impractical to write every word of the psych book on my head, so I opted for rereading the chapters until I was able to locate any topic I needed on its exact page.

I was in the middle of chapter three when the phone rang. It was Stanley. John's words came flooding back – *He's going to call you tomorrow.*

Stanley said, "John Levy gave me your name. Did he tell you?"

"Yes, back in June." I said.

"Isn't it still June?" he quipped.

"I don't know about you, but I just celebrated Labor Day. I'm pretty sure that's in September."

"How about that! Time has a way of getting out of hand, doesn't it? In any event, I'd like to take you out for dinner."

"Okay. Next weekend starts the high holy days; do you want to wait till after that?"

"Not particularly. I don't care if you don't care."

"I'm not religious either, so it's fine with me."

"Well, why don't we meet Friday after work?"

"All right. I'll drive in and meet you. Tell me where you work."

"Drive in? I thought you worked in Manhattan."

"No, that must be some other name you got from John. Possibly Susan from CBS or Carol from Connecticut. I'm Joan from Jersey."

"You're the very first person I called on this long list."

“I don’t believe it. After three months?”

“I was too busy mowing the lawn to date anyone.” I giggled.

“So where do you work?”

“In the General Motors building.”

“I know that place,” I said. “I was at the Auto Pub. It was like being at a drive-in movie. We had so much fun sitting at a table, built like a car, watching movies on a screen set in front of us. I bet you’ve eaten there often.”

“That’s where I work,” he said.

“At the Auto Pub?”

“I’m a waiter there.”

“No you’re not.” (I didn’t believe him.)

“Yes I am.” (I still didn’t believe him.)

“Well, just tell me where you want to meet and where to park the car.”

“No need to worry about that. I’ll come to New Jersey.”

"I'd rather just meet you in New York, really." It was common knowledge that first date meetings with strangers should be in a public place where escape from groping fingers and smooching lips is possible.

"That's not my way. I'll pick you up and take you home. I don't want you driving into New York."

Negotiations continued until I was forced to concede. We spent the next thirty minutes telling each other stories that made us laugh. He complained that women didn't get his sense of humor.

"I was on a dinner date," he said, "and a bit of vegetable fell from my fork onto the floor. I pointed to the ground and asked her, 'You know what we have here, don't you?' She stared at me blankly. I looked her straight in the eye and said, 'Peas on earth, of course.'"

I've always loved puns ever since I saw a quote on a cocktail napkin which read, "It is better to have loved a short man, than never to have loved a tall." So I knew he'd appreciate my story about the Spanish teacher who asked the class, "What do you think the word *Dudar* means?" She hinted that it sounded very much like its English counterpart. "The Camptown Races," I answered. "You know,

The Camptown ladies sign this song, Dudar, Dudar." Stanley appreciated the retort even if the teacher did not.

Later, I told a friend that I didn't want to meet Stanley because I had a good thing going with him on the phone.

*****

Our first date was switched from Friday to Saturday September 9th, for Stan's driving convenience. Refusing to listen to directions, he subsequently took the longest possible route from Long Island to Fairlawn. He drove through the midtown tunnel, navigated Manhattan's congested streets, and reached New Jersey via the Lincoln Tunnel, rather than traveling across the George Washington Bridge which led directly to my town.

I was still planning on moving to Florida. My downstairs rooms were jam-packed with boxes, along with garage sale items. A single bedspring and mattress was prominently displayed awaiting pickup: quite a sight for Stanley as he entered the dining room. Not that I cared. I had no intention of getting involved, although I did dress and primp to look my best. I wasn't going to put on any *first-date* airs. If I allowed myself to just be me, he wouldn't find that compelling enough to come back.

160

I offered him my favorite drink, Galliano and orange juice, and left him standing next to a knick-knack covered dining table with just enough space for a glass on a coaster. I ran upstairs to grab my purse. I stuffed it with a credit card and cash in case things got rough.

He was less than enthusiastic about the drink and gladly handed it to me practically untouched. "I'm not much of a drinker," he said.

"Neither am I," I confessed. "I only drink this because it tastes like a Creamsicle."

"I like your decorative touches. The mattress gives the place a sense of spontaneity and movement."

"I'm moving to Florida," I said.

"Really? Looks like you planned to move yesterday."

"Very funny! We better leave! I don't want to be late for our reservation." I poured the contents of his glass in the sink as I pushed him out the door.

My friend suggested a restaurant a few towns away. In the car, our conversation centered on directions - turn here, turn there, go straight. Stanley's response to each directive was either,

"O.K." or "Are you sure you know where you're going?" To which I always replied, "No."

Too bad GPS hadn't been invented.

I gasped as we entered the restaurant. It was fancier than I had expected. The walls surrounding the dining area had museum-quality paintings, each one centered on a mahogany panel, and separated by a wood column, painted in mustard gold. A fireplace graced one of the walls with several lit candles on the mantel.

I looked at Stanley for a reaction. He was poised and unperturbed. He asked the tuxedoed Maître d' for our reservation. We followed a runner to our table. He placed napkins on our laps and handed us the menu. I watched as Stanley read through the evening offerings without so much as a shudder at the prices. We declined the sommelier's invitation to bring us the perfect wine to go with our porterhouse steaks. I rethought my earlier negation of formality and opted for a more restrained demeanor, especially regarding table manners and polite conversation.

Then a quarter of the way through dinner, Stanley heaved a sigh indicating that he was getting full. He lifted his fork in the air, made large circles in front of his face, added airplane noises along with the loops and landed the food in his mouth as one would do with a toddler in a high chair. I laughed out loud, which delighted Stanley and encouraged his humor to surface more fully. The rest of the evening flowed effortlessly.

After our dinner was charged on his golden American Express card, Stanley asked, "Would you like to go somewhere to dance?" *All this on a waiter's salary? Ha!* I thought.

"Sure, why not?" I had no idea where to go. We drove around until I saw a sign for Fort Lee and remembered there was a bar at the foot of the George Washington Bridge. I heard that it had a band and a dance floor. We arrived around 9:30. The place turned out to be a dive. There was a scattering of patrons drinking, talking, and happily listening to juke box music. We found a table and sat down. There was a two drink minimum to stay seated. They didn't have Galliano, so we ordered four Screwdrivers, clicked glasses and made a toast to the future. We took one sip before the band came back. They started the session with "A Long Cool Woman in a Black Dress." Stan pulled me onto the dance floor; we didn't sit down till the band stopped playing. The vodka and orange juice followed the Galliano down the drain.

We arrived at my door around midnight. Stanley suggested he stay the night as it was a long ride home and he was tired. I declined the offer, but happily recommended a faster way home, which he ignored. "Call me when you get home, so I know you made it," I said. He kissed me goodnight, sulked his way down the steps, slid into the car with a sigh, and drove off.

*****

The doorbell rang the following Wednesday morning. "Flower delivery, ma'am," the young man said, placing the vase in my hand.

"For me?"

"S'pose so, Ma'am."

"Who sent them?"

"Don't rightly know, Ma'am. The card's inside the envelope there. See it?"

"Hold on a minute. I want to give you something." I brought the flowers into the house and set them on a table. I found a dollar in my purse. When I handed it to him, he tipped his cap, smiled, and said, "Welcome, Ma'am."

It wasn't my birthday, so I checked the address to be sure the flowers were meant for me. Joan Morris – 11 Arlington Place, Fair Lawn, NJ. "Who's sending me flowers?" I wondered. I opened the gift card. It read:

"Dear Susan,

Now table # 7 doesn't have any flowers on it anymore,

Love, the Waiter."

When Stanley told me he was a waiter during our first telephone conversation, I was determined to find out the truth. I called a friend who worked three blocks from the General Motors building. He searched the directory in the lobby, found his name, called the company, and asked for Stanley's exact title which was Treasurer of the Dreyfus Corporation.

Stanley called that evening. "I thought you were going to call me when you got home," I said.

"I just got home," he said.

"Thanks for the flowers. I loved the note. Where do you really work?" I asked. He was not ready to share that information, but asked me for a second date, the one we spent at the Jersey shore.

A prospective marriage was looking more advantageous than Florida. The stakes were higher. I wanted this relationship to work. No more joking around. It was time to be serious. On our next phone call, I was solemn, steering the conversation to worldly matters, keeping a somber, intellectual air. It wasn't long before he rebelled. "Are you feeling all right?" he asked.

"Yes, of course, why do you ask?"

"You seemed to have lost your sense of humor."

"Hold on a minute. I'll go look for it." I don't remember the conversation after that except a third date was set for me to drive to Stanley's house with Michael and Jenny on Saturday. On Friday night, at dinner with my parents, I formulated a scheme to level the playing field of humor.

*****

"Huntington?" my friend responded when I told her where Stanley lived. "That's a very wealthy community. He must be rich."

"He may be," I said. "He lives on a street called Upper Drive."

"Bet it overlooks the Long Island Sound!"

"Do you really think so?" I was excited at the prospect.

A wrong turn on the expressway put me on Southern Parkway leading to the south shore of Long Island. At the time, I was unaware that I had driven twenty miles out of my way. I exited on Rte. 110, following Stan's directions, and made the long drive back to the north shore. When I reached Huntington, I began to look for the mountainous road with a house overlooking the Sound. The flat terrain never changed as I zigzagged my way through the streets and avenues. The final turn was into a development of small houses. I pulled up to a ranch house with an orange garage door and matching shutters. The mailbox at the foot of the driveway displayed two large brass numbers announcing I had arrived at 14 Upper Drive. *You've got to be kidding. What happened to my friend's promise of Huntington is a wealthy community? Wait till I get my hands on her!*

I was greeted warmly by Stanley and his brood. At noon, we sat at the kitchen table and made sandwiches from the egg and tuna salad left in the refrigerator by their housekeeper. The Fausts talked about how she came into their lives and how much they hated her.

Around 1:00 p.m. the phone rang. Stan answered.

"Is this Mr. Stanley Faust?" a male voice asked.

"Yes, what can I do for you?"

"This is Brooks Moving Company. We want to check your address. Do you live at 14 Upper Drive?"

"Yes. But what is this all about?"

"We wanted to be sure someone was there to receive the furniture."

"The furniture? What furniture?"

"The bill of lading says we're to bring the contents of the home of Joan Morris to 14 Upper Drive."

"Sure," Stanley chuckled, "Bring it on over." He grabbed me and gave me a big bear hug. "That was great," he said, "really great."

I had to convince my father to be a co-conspirator in the prank. He didn't understand the nature of our relationship. It was clear by now that our attraction for one another was linked to humor.

✳✳✳✳✳

Three days later on, October 4th, while making lunch for the kids, the phone rang. It was Stan. "What are you doing tonight?

"Nothing, why do you ask?"

"I want to come out."

"On a Wednesday night? Don't you have to be home for your kids?"

"The housekeeper is with them. I have a surprise for you."

"Good, I love surprises. What is it?"

"You'll see tonight. Get a baby sitter."

Our fourth date was spent at a Chinese restaurant, three blocks from my house. After we ordered, without saying a word, Stanley made a big show of digging in one pocket after the other, without coming up with anything. With each pocket search, his facial expression grew more and more frantic. "Oh, well," he said with a shrug, "Next time." Before I could formulate my thoughts to respond to his actions, he cut me off and bantered about his amazing day at work until our plates were empty. He asked the waiter to bring the check, at which point he reached into the very pocket he had first looked in and handed me two ring boxes. "Will you marry me?"

I didn't answer the question; I was too curious about the boxes. I flipped them open.

"Why two diamond rings?" I asked.

"I wanted you to pick the one you liked best."

I slid the marquis on first and then the pear-shaped diamond, all the while thinking how important and wealthy Stanley must be for a jeweler to allow him to take two diamonds out of the store. He must have left some form of collateral with the jeweler. Nevertheless, I was impressed.

"Are these real diamonds? I asked.

"Just pick the one you like best. I'll bring the other one back tomorrow."

"I like the pear-shaped one," I said, knowing that his response answered the question. I placed the other box in his hand, letting the diamond sparkle in his eyes.

"I guess that means you've accepted my proposal."

"Not until my parents approve. Let's have dinner with them Saturday night. You can ask my father for my hand in marriage. It will be fun."

I called my parents the next morning and told them to have Hedy, their housekeeper, prepare a nice meal for Saturday night, that Stan had proposed and I accepted, but that he was going to ask Father for my hand.

*****

The Faust family arrived Saturday around 4:00 for our fifth date: we were expected at my parents place at 6:00. We left the kids alone in the house while Stan and I went for a walk. "I have something to tell you," he said, with his bad boy face. I nodded. "It's not a real diamond; it's cubic zirconia, but it looks real doesn't it?"

"It sure does," I agreed, "and even better." He gave me a quizzical look. "It doesn't cost as much, and I won't feel badly if I lose it." He smiled. "I promise it will be our secret," I said, and put my arm through his. Stan's shoulders softened and he picked up the pace. When we arrived home, we found Lori in my roller skates, gliding across the living room floor, David and Michael in the den watching television in silence, and Jenny and Robert on the floor playing Monopoly. The baby sitter arrived at 5:30 and we headed out.

*****

I introduced Stan to my parents, and they couldn't be more gracious. The anticipation of my remarrying and settling down was more thrilling than their trip to India to see the Taj Mahal. His position as treasurer in a big company far exceeded their expectations for their flighty daughter. Father finally had a prospective son-in-law with whom he could discuss finances, politics, and the state of the economy. Mother was overjoyed to have a son-in-law about whom she could boast.

The conversation was lively during dinner, but by the time dessert was served, Stan still had not mentioned the subject at hand. With a mixture of boldness and timidity, I leaned across the table and asked Stanley, "Didn't you have something you wanted to ask my father?" He gave me a blank stare, looked quizzically at my father, and shrugged his shoulders as he faced my mother. I panicked. *Did I misunderstand his intentions?* My parents stared at me downright bewildered as to what the hell was going on. "Oh yes," Stan said, "Mr. Gruber, may I have your daughter's hand in marriage?" It was the only prank Stan pulled that didn't get a laugh out of me.

✳✳✳✳✳

We decided to wed on October 21, 1972, which acted as our date, six weeks after we met. I don't remember why the hurry. Perhaps, since Stan's first wife died of cancer, he wasn't taking any chances of losing his new found love by waiting any longer than necessary.

I suggested that we just move in together, nuptials be hanged! But Stan was an old fashioned, upstanding citizen and refused to entertain such a radical idea.

I had two weeks to obtain a Rabbi, choose a bridal venue, assemble a guest list, send invitations, select a menu, order a wedding cake, obtain a band, purchase flowers, buy an appropriate third marriage ensemble, unearth matching dresses for my bridesmaids, Lori and Jenny (which they both hated), purchase two suits for Michael and David, the groomsmen, and one for Robert, the ring bearer. Thankfully, Stan was on his own to choose his attire.

My childhood Rabbi was available to perform the ceremony, as he did twice before. Stan said he would walk down the aisle with a placard on his back with the number three on it. Telephone calls replaced the formal invitation. The banquet hall of our dreams turned out to be a meeting hall on the lower level of an office building where forty-eight of us sipped wine and nibbled on hors d'oeuvres before the ceremony, dined on roast beef, sat around five tables centered with a bouquet of yellow and orange chrysanthemums and marigolds to match the décor of the room, and danced to the music of an accordion/guitar player. The formal, four-tiered cake was the only clue that this was a wedding celebration.

Stan and I spent our wedding night at the Saddle Brook Marriot Hotel. Our honeymoon in Mexico had to wait till the following summer.

Hats Off to a Slow Start

On October 21, 1972, at the age of 33, I married Stanley, a widower with three children: twelve-year-old David, eleven-year-old Lori, and five-year-old Robert.

I didn't come into the marriage empty handed either. I brought my eight-year-old daughter, Jenny, from a previous marriage. My son, Michael, was living with his father at the time.

Thus began our not-so-*Brady Bunch* life together. Being a mother seemed natural enough, and I never gave it much thought, but I had the impression that being a stepmother was somewhat different. Would it be like wearing two different hats, or was motherhood and stepmotherhood the opposite sides of the same coin?

I knew the pitfalls. A new wife might overstep her bounds in disciplining her husband's children. I might treat my own child more favorably than my stepchildren. I may find it easier to observe and criticize the faults of these relative strangers than my own offspring.

I was determined to be as perfect a stepmother as I could. I began by asking my husband what his wishes were on a specific topic before approaching his children about it. For instance, "David doesn't want to eat breakfast before he goes to school. Should I make him?"

Reply: "David should eat breakfast."

Me: "I agree that he should eat breakfast. But should I *make him* eat breakfast?"

Reply: "David should eat breakfast."

On another occasion the question was, "What time do you want the kids to go to bed on a school night?"

"I don't know. Whatever time you think they should is all right with me."

Then there was this question. "May the kids go to their friend's house to play after school, or do you want them to do their homework first?"

"Whatever you think best, sweetheart."

Thus I became the one and only disciplinarian. However, I was a lenient parent. I said yes to almost any request unless I thought it involved something harmful or dangerous.

I never criticized David, Lori, or Robert, and bent over backwards to treat them the same way I treated Jenny.

Three months into the marriage, Lori was sitting at the kitchen table while I was doing the dishes. She asked, "If I tell you something, promise me that you won't get mad."

"I promise," I said.

"You know, you don't treat us the same way you treat Jenny." My heart sank. I was sure that I had been the consummate stepmother – kind, gentle, loving, balanced, fair, giving, helpful, supportive, and above all, accommodating.

I sat down beside her. "I'm not angry. In fact, I'm glad you told me. I was totally unaware that I've been treating you differently than Jenny. In fact, sweetheart, if you hadn't told me about this, there would be no way to change the situation and correct whatever's wrong."

"Well," she continued, "Whenever you don't like something we do, you sit us down and talk to us about it. But when Jenny does something that you don't like, you give her a quick slap on the backside."

What a shock. I had no idea I was doing that. Turns out I was being a better stepmother than a mother. *Who would have thunk!*

There was only one thing to do. Any time Jenny misbehaved after that, I'd take a moment to ask myself *what I would do if this were Lori?* That worked. I became a better parent thanks to the insight of my eleven-year-old stepdaughter.

Our First Fight

"All right, go ahead. Invite the Lindbergs and the Johnstones!"

It was the middle of the night, and my husband decided to reopen the discussion played out earlier in the evening.

"No, that's okay," I mumbled, pulling the covers over my shoulders.

"No, you're right," he persisted, and moved closer to me, which caused the cover to slip from my shoulder into the crevice. "You *should* invite the Lindbergs and the Johnstones."

I yanked the blanket from under his torso, and wrapped it around my shoulder. "Honey, it really doesn't matter."

"Yes, it does! I'm sorry I gave you a hard time. I shouldn't have told you not to invite them."

"It's okay, sweetheart. I appreciate your apology. I love you," I said, holding in my frustration. I readjusted myself into a more comfortable position. There was a moment of silence.

"So are you going to invite them or not?"

"If you want me to, I will," I said, "but why don't we talk about it in the morning?" I was under the impression that I could end this discussion and get back to sleep.

"Well, I just wanted you to know that it was all right with me if you invited the Lindbergs and the Johnstones."

"Thank you, honey, I love you very much. Sleep well and pleasant dreams."

*****

We had been married for a little over a month. It was his second marriage, and my third. I moved into his house and, under my guidance, his children were planning a party in honor of our marriage, so I could meet the neighbors. The children supplied the guest list, which included my husband's acquaintances as well as the parents of their own friends. They were looking forward to my meeting everyone. But my husband vetoed the Lindbergs and the Johnstones because he did not know them very well. "I have nothing in common with them," he said.

I maintained that since the children were eager for me to meet everyone on the list, we shouldn't disappoint them. "It's a perfect opportunity for you to get to know them better," I said.

Ultimately, their names were crossed off the list.

*****

I was just dozing off again when I felt my husband's arm go around my waist. He kissed me on the cheek, and heaved a deep sigh. I ignored it. He kissed me again. I ignored it again. I kept hoping that he would go back to sleep, and let me do likewise. But my wishes were in vain. "I hate it when I give you a hard time," he whispered. "I shouldn't have given you a hard time. I shouldn't have said anything about not inviting the Lindbergs and the Johnstones."

"It's okay," I said, trying hard to control my irritation. "Let's just forget the whole thing. It's not important." I tried desperately to end this ridiculous dialogue, and get some sleep. We both lay still for a while, and I thought it was over, and it might have been, if the gods weren't against me. I became aware of the need to use the bathroom. Oh, how I didn't want to get up. I tried not to think about it. But the more I tried to disregard my need, the more urgent it became. So against my better judgment, yet not having much choice, I got up and left the room.

I walked as quietly as I could to and from the bathroom, and slipped softly onto the bed, and gently under the covers. Everything was quiet. Everything was still. Could this be it, I wondered. Is it over? Good, now maybe I can get to sleep!

But that was not to be. My heart was pounding, my mind was racing, my body was filled with tension, and my eyes were wide open. I tried lying still for what seemed an eternity while I searched my mind for one of those "never-fail" relaxation exercises.

I was at war with myself. The part of me that was angry would not let the part of me that wanted to sleep find peace. The struggle within produced an uncontrollable scream, *Aaargh*, and I knew I was doomed.

"What's the matter, sweetheart?" my husband responded ever so innocently to my outburst.

You know damn well what the matter is, I thought. But I held my tongue, and said, as calmly as possible, "Nothing, sweetheart. I'm just having a little trouble falling back to sleep."

"Are you upset with me?"

Another naïve question, I thought, and the irritation burst forth. "Well, I just don't see why you had to wake me up in the middle of the night to discuss such a stupid subject."

"I didn't wake you. You were up."

"I wasn't up. I just turned over in my sleep."

"Well, I thought you were up!"

"Well, I wasn't!"

"I thought you would be happy to know that I changed my mind about the Lindbergs and the Johnstones."

"Not at two in the morning!"

"I'm sorry. It was just on my mind, and I couldn't sleep."

"So you decided that I shouldn't sleep either!"

"I said I was sorry," and then in that little naughty boy voice of his, he added, "Please forgive me, cause I love you, and I'm really, really sorry."

"Okay, I forgive you," I replied, even though I was still churning inside. "And I love you too," I said, although I didn't feel the love very strongly at the moment. "Good night," I added, wanting to end this entire affair once and for all.

But I still couldn't sleep. The adrenaline was flowing wildly through my body. I got out of bed, and headed for the kitchen. I had left the dinner dishes in the sink, and thought that doing them now might discharge some of that pent-up energy. I began banging one dish after the other into the dishwasher, trying desperately to rid myself of the anger. I wiped the counter with fury, and shoved the chairs under the table. I grabbed the broom and swept the floor with quick, agitated strokes.

Out of the corner of my eye, I saw my husband come in and sit at the far end of the table near the door. He didn't say anything. I kept sweeping. He sat there without a word. I swept without a word. He seemed calm and amused. I lacked composure.

Finally, I couldn't take the silence any longer. "What do you want?" I bellowed.

"Nothing," he grinned. "I just thought I would get up and mow the lawn."

One-of-a-Kind Girl Scout Badge

As leader of Troop 243 in Huntington, Long Island, I took six Girl Scouts on a special day trip, a reward for earning their assigned badges. My co-leader got sick at the last minute. Having remarried six months prior, I was a new resident to the area, and unaware of the traffic I would encounter. We were further delayed by my ignorance of the complex ferry scheduling.

When I finally reached the ticket master, we were told that we had just missed the boat to Ocean Beach, and we'd have to wait an hour for the next one.

"Why so long?"

"Ma'am, we have a planned schedule for the boats. We service seven different locations on Fire Island."

"Should we take the boat that's leaving now, and walk to Ocean Beach?"

"Sure, but it's a half hour walk along the beach from there. If you don't want to wait here for an hour, you and the scouts could swim across if you like!"

"Thanks. We'll take the boat." To make matters worse, credit cards weren't accepted, and I didn't have enough cash. I had to borrow money from the scouts for the seven round trip tickets.

Once on shore, I spied a Tony Curtis look-alike dressed in a navy-blue sports coat, white trousers, a button-down shirt, which was left opened to reveal his well-developed chest, and the cleanest white shoes I've ever seen, not unlike the playboy outfit worn by Tony in *Some Like It Hot* in his pursuit to seduce Marilyn Monroe.

I asked him to show me the path to the beach. "Follow me," he said, with a wide grin; his eyes sparkled in the bright sunshine. He asked me about our trip, and why I didn't take the ferry directly to Ocean Beach. I explained our plight, and he gave rapt attention to my every word. It was a heavenly change from my husband's usual response, *What? Would you mind repeating that?* He advised us to stay along the shoreline because it would be easier to walk where the sand was wet and firmly packed. He told us to be careful, have a good time, and look for the beautiful boats that pass along the shore. He winked at me and waved goodbye; his essence stayed in my thought. I was ripe for a love fantasy.

The scouts removed their shoes and socks at the water's edge and left the noisy dock area behind.

We jumped in and out of the waves in rhythm to the ebb and flow of the water. As we walked, the beach became less and less crowded until it was dotted with a single sunbather every fifty feet or so, and farther up on the sand, with a couple lying so close together that, from a distance, they looked like human Love Bugs.

All of a sudden one of the girls shouted, "That man doesn't have any clothes on."

"Don't look at him. Turn away," I said.

A second girl yelled, "Those guys are sitting there without bathing suits."

"Girls," I said. "From now on keep your eyes on the ocean. Watch for the boats that nice man told us about."

Why would a public beach allow nude sunbathing? They must know people walk along the beach?"

I felt a tug on my arm and looked down. "Mrs. Faust, can I ask you something?"

"Sure, Lizzie. EYES ON THE WATER, GIRLS."

"Do you know where we docked today?"

"Cherry Grove. Why?"

"That's what I thought," she said furrowing her brows.

"Why do you ask?"

"I think I heard my parents say something about it being a place where gay men go."

"Oh my God, oh my God. EYES ON THE WATER, GIRLS. Do you mean EVERYONE there is gay?"

"I don't know. Maybe. I guess so."

"LOOK AT THAT BEAUTIFUL SAIL BOAT, GIRLS."

"We're looking Mrs. Faust, we're all looking," one girl yelled back, laughing with her arms around her friends as they ran, splashing each other with their feet.

"What have I done?" I lamented.

"Don't worry, Mrs. Faust, most of us have brothers. We know what boys look like," said Lizzie.

"That's a relief, but what about the girls who don't have brothers?"

"Maybe they can earn a badge for learning something new?" She giggled.

I hurried the girls along. I had been told not to let the girls on the dunes, but had no idea what a dune was. But there were these wonderful mountains of sand lining the beach which looked like a lot of fun. The girls climbed up and slid back down the mounds until a patrol officer approached and shouted, "Girls, get down from there." Looking straight at me he asked, "Ma'am, what do you think you're doing?"

"What do you mean?" I retorted.

"Why are you allowing the girls to play on the dunes? Sand dunes are very important to the coastal ecosystem. They keep the beaches safe from erosion and should not be played upon by careless visitors."

"Sorry officer," I said with a repentant look. "I didn't realize." I bowed my head to hide the tears forming in my eyes.

I led the girls away from the scene of the crime to a picnic area to lunch and play while I sat alone. I thought this day away from my husband would be a special treat for me. We were having trouble adjusting to each other's ways. He had lost his first wife to cancer, and was insistent that we do everything together. I felt smothered by his fear of losing me.

We headed for the dock to catch the ferry back. The tears remained in my eyes as we drove home. I regretted missing the boat and exposing the scouts to the nude beach. I was feeling guilty about my faux pas on the dunes and embarrassed about being confronted by an officer. But most of the tears were for my misapprehension about the handsome stranger, for the fool I made of myself by thinking he was flirting with me, and most of all, for buying into the fantasy of love and romance.

The Days of My Adoption

I accompanied my daughter, Jennifer, to Russia to adopt Jaclynn. The following is what I imagined this three-year-old girl thinking and was written as a class assignment on point of view.

The last time I heard Russian spoken was the day I left the big, old, wobbly *Dome*. That is what we called the orphanage where I lived ever since I can remember. Each child there was waiting to be adopted. When that happened, a party with cake and ice cream was given to celebrate the happy occasion. But it didn't make me happy to know I would never see my playmates again. I wouldn't cry. Instead, I would run outside to the playground and jump on one of the swings. I'd swing and swing and swing, faster and faster and faster, higher and higher and higher until my heart stopped hurting. Most of the time I just kept swinging until one of the caretakers had to come out, pull me from the swing, and take me inside.

One day, when I was 3 ½ years old, two people arrived at the dome to adopt me: my new mama and a lady whom I called Babushka. Babushka called my new mama Jennifer. She was very pretty, with long blonde hair, and a nose that looked like a button on my pajamas, and I loved to touch it. They brought me new clothes, a miniature stuffed horse, a coloring book and crayons. We were brought to a room where we spent all day together playing. I grabbed the dress I liked best to put on. Babushka helped me because I tried to put it on over the clothes I was wearing. I was having so much fun that I kept forgetting to go to the bathroom, and one dress after another got wet, until I was wearing the last new dress. Babushka had gone off to find a bathroom after they put me into the second dress, but she couldn't find it. I could have told them where it was if they had asked me in Russian. Finally, Mama went in search of a caretaker who took me to the bathroom and put all the wet clothes in a basket to be washed. After that I stayed dry.

I peeled the paper from the crayons. Babushka showed me how to color with them, but I liked peeling the paper better. My new mama seemed shy and not quite sure how to play with me, but she enjoyed watching us, and joined in when we started tossing a ball around.

Later in the day, we were told to go into the pediatrician's office. I hid behind a desk and then jumped up and yelled, "Babushka!" That was the first time I called her Babushka, and she loved it. I was surprised she understood what the word meant. When the pediatrician arrived, she said that my new family had to leave, but they would be back in three months' time. I asked why they couldn't take me now.

"There is a lot of paper work to do," she said. I didn't know what that meant, but before I could find out, a caretaker came to take me to dinner. Mama got permission for me to keep for my very own the stuffed horse and the dress I was wearing, and not be obligated to share it with the other children, which is what happened to all the clothes that were dumped in the laundry. Mama and Babushka gave me hugs and kisses before I left. I walked out of the room in my new dress, clutching my horse.

Three months seemed like a very long time, and I thought they would never come back. But sure enough, on August 31, 2004, they arrived to take me to a place called America.

Mama gave me a new outfit and a pair of patent leather shoes to wear for our trip. Babushka took a video of her trying to get me dressed. She yelled instructions to Mama from behind the camera. It was the first time Mama ever had to dress a little child, and she struggled to get my feet into the shoes.

I was happy that I had a new family, but when the moving box, called a van, headed down the hill from the only home I ever knew, my stomach pinched me so hard that I almost cried, and I felt like there was a yoyo stuck in my throat. Part of me longed to be swinging in the playground. I had never been *in* the van before or farther than the top of the driveway. My heart skipped and hopped as the van turned onto another road. I lost my balance and tumbled to the floor. I began to cry. Babushka picked me up and held me close to her bosom. I didn't feel the jumping of the van anymore. She pointed out the window at things passing by and said words I did not know: tree – sign – car – flower – truck – grass – train. She repeated the same word every time she pointed to the same thing. We passed a big, long yellow box on wheels. There were children inside looking out of the windows. Babushka pointed to it and said, "Bus."

I said, "Buth."

"Buss," my mama said, and laughed.

"Buth," I said, and laughed.

"Bussss," Babushka said, and we all laughed some more.

They tried to get me to say other strange words. But, I liked saying "buth," and I said it every time I saw one, until the van stopped and we got out.

We went into a big, noisy place with lots of people moving about. There were men and women in uniforms with gold stripes on their sleeves, and wings on their jackets. My hand was held tightly as we walked quickly from one place to another. Then we put our bags and packages on a long moving table which carried them inside something that looked like a giant barrel lying on its side without a top or bottom on it. A man made us walk through a tall opening with flashing lights.

Then we picked up the things from the other end of the barrel and carried them to a big room with lots of chairs and couches. When we found an empty couch, we dropped everything on the floor and sat down. I turned to Babushka and said, "ca-ca." She grabbed my hand and took me to the bathroom. I was relieved that Babushka understood where I had to go.

I saw a glass-front machine that had candy, chips, and cookies inside, and pointed to a familiar treat, and said, "Dietaya." Mama looked shocked. Later, I found out that she thought I said, *die to ya'*, but I was only asking her to 'give me' in Russian. She dropped rubles into the machine and out came a *Mishka Na Severe*.

"Vkusno," I said, gobbling down the candy.

I walked around the room and asked, "govorit' po-Russki?" If they answered "Da," I sat down next to them, and had a conversation.

All of a sudden, everyone in the room lined up, and walked thru a small door into an area with lots of seats in long rows. I lay down across one of the seats, and immediately fell asleep. I slept until we had to walk through the tiny door again into a large building that looked just like the one we were in before. But everyone in this building said the same funny words used by my new family. It's called English.

Not Me!

I'm not prejudiced, I tell myself. *And I'm certainly not racist.*

In February of 2017, I listen to NPR and hear about increased hate crimes. How fear and anxiety is sweeping the country. I listen to the plights of Muslims, African-Americans, and Latinos. As a theater buff, I see plays and films about minorities who struggle to overcome so many stumbling blocks. After viewing *I Am Not Your Negro*, a documentary based on the words of James Baldwin, I feel overwhelmed by the film's revelations on my innocent and naïve thoughts. I learn of the depth and far-reaching consequences of the systemic action of our country which allows "justice for all" for mostly white, wealthy men, a state of affairs which has been fought against throughout the years, but is currently on the rise again.

A woman stands up and announces, "If you would like to know more about this cause, please come and speak with me." I don't grasp what she is saying. I'm thinking there might be a *talk back* in another room where I can sit passively and listen, without sharing. She has information about organizations that fight against racism and requests my e-mail address. I'm flustered. After a moment of silence, she introduces herself as Maeve and we start to converse. She is a young white Jewish woman who was brought up in New York and is an active member in the European Dissent/White Anti-Racist Group. "I'll be happy to send you some websites to research, without commitment on your part," she says, and I surrender my e-mail.

On my walk home, I feel ambivalent about becoming an activist. The liberal part of me wants to help; the selfish part of me definitely does not. After connecting a few more times with Maeve, I agree to join her at their April meeting.

*****

In their musical *South Pacific*, Rodgers and Hammerstein write a song that sums up how the seeds of prejudice are planted and cultivated to take root in the minds of the young.

You've got to be taught to hate and fear,

You've got to be taught from year to year,

It's got to be drummed in your dear little ear--

You've got to be carefully taught!

You've got to be taught to be afraid

Of people whose eyes are oddly made,

And people whose skin is a different shade

You've got to be carefully taught.

You've got to be taught before it's too late,

Before you are six or seven or eight,

To hate all the people your relatives hate--

You've got to be carefully taught!

I was not overtly taught to hate or fear. I come from a liberal home environment. Our family is a member of the Jewish minority. Both my parents grew up with modest means. My father is a self-made man, so I'm born into a family of wealth and into the arms of Lena, a combination housekeeper/nanny who is African-American. In 1939, the year she arrives in our home, she is referred to as "colored." This is the word I remember. I love her. My older sister tells me how she enjoyed siting in the basement with Lena as she did the laundry and ironing. Lena is our go-to person, reliable, helpful and kind. I wonder when I became aware that her skin was a different shade than mine, and less desirable. It is never mentioned. Lena is considered a part of the family. Yet, somewhere along the way, certainly before the age of seven or eight, I recall my sister and I having a conversation about how we might go about turning Lena's black skin to white. I'm not clear on whether we came up with this idea ourselves or read it in a book. It involves having her sit in a tub of bleach. Was this a kind of prejudice, or a child's act of love, or both? I wonder how Lena, or Brownie, or Hedy, or the other African-American women who worked in our home felt about us.

I hold the image of travelling to Newark to shop for school clothes with mother and looking for a place to have lunch. I'm about 11. As we reach the door to a restaurant, she turns around and says this is not a good choice. I ask her why. "Because there are coloreds eating there, so it can't be very good," she says. It is the first and last time I remember a comment about African-Americans ever being mentioned. Yet, it leaves an immediate and lasting impression on my mind. I'm curious about the statement. But I don't question the validity of it. Nor do I understand the connection between coloreds and the quality of food. Why would different skin colors affect the taste of food? Lena is an excellent cook, and we certainly enjoy her preparations. I'm still too young to see the economic differences between people and the quality of establishments. Perhaps this awareness is behind Mother's viewpoint.

As a young adult in a changing world, mother's admonition rings in my ears whenever I enter a restaurant. I fight back. I chide myself, acknowledging the absence of truth in the very thought. I open the door and walk in. I welcome the equality. After a while, I stop noticing the mix of blacks and whites in a restaurant, and that initial response disappears.

*****

Blacks are the minority in our high school class of 1957, comprising only 6% out of the 215 student body. With 29% of the class being Jewish, 22% being Italian, and 43% being a mix of other European countries, it breaks down to exactly 12 black students in our class, five of whom I know because they are enrolled in the Academic Program, the same as I. Harold, who is a Mechanical Arts student, sits in back of me in homeroom, and we consider ourselves friends. He and I share the same sense of humor and make each other laugh. But I don't inquire about his home life in the black section of town, and he knows nothing about my upper class home life.

Many of my friends and I consider two of the black students good looking, one male and one female. We want these two to get together and date, and suggest to Virginia she date Brent. I wonder if this is a form of racism. I wonder if we disrespected them by suggesting it.

Obviously, my contact with the African-American community is very limited, and perhaps that's why I don't see the schism between the races even though, as a freshman, I become aware of economic differences by the difference in homes and neighborhoods in which my classmates live. This awareness does not affect my choice of acquaintances or friends. We all dress much the same. The designer craze occurs many years in the future and everyone I know gets the same ten dollar allowance every week, or, at least, has the funds to pay for whatever it is we want to do. I am totally oblivious to the world outside of my own teenage life.

When I'm a sophomore and sixteen years old, Rosa Parks is arrested for refusing to move to the back of the bus in Montgomery, Alabama. The news about the Civil Rights movement is on television every night. I root for Rosa and watch with horror at the violence of the white community. I celebrate the bus boycott ending a year later.

I'm racing through my life during the Civil Rights movement. I graduate high school, go to college, get married, have a baby, get divorced, remarry, have a second child, get divorced again, and go back to college. I empathize with the movement, but it never occurs to me to advocate for the black community. I'm too busy finding my own way through this complicated life.

*****

On April 11, 1968, President Lyndon Johnson signs the Civil Rights Act prohibiting discrimination in the sale, rental, and financing of housing. I rejoice. I'm asked to participate in a local commercial to publicize the new law. I play a real estate broker who says, "I don't discriminate. I just keep our neighborhoods free of undesirables." The voiceover asserts that *is* discrimination. After it airs, I'm frightened that someone will gun me down, believing I'm a legitimate realtor.

*****

I think of the time I inadvertently offended an African-American woman when on jury duty. We are to fill out forms, which I neglect to do. The woman in question tells me her card is already complete. I say, "Oh, you're a good girl!" She becomes incensed. "Don't call me girl." I immediately apologize and explain that my sister and I say that to each other whenever one of us does something right and the other doesn't. I apologize again and say I meant no harm. I knew that calling a black man "boy" was disrespectful, but never extended the concept to calling a black woman a girl.

*****

I marry Stanley in 1972 and move into his bi-racial neighborhood in Huntington, Long Island, NY. My daughter, Jenny, has an African-American friend, Tracy. When Jenny invites her to join the family on an outing to Sunken Meadow State Park, Stanley objects. We fight about it. Never having gone to that beach before, I'm not certain it wouldn't be a problem, but I want to take a stand. He wins, or perhaps I let him win, being indecisive, leaving my daughter sad and angry. Later that summer, Tracy invites Jenny and me to her home to swim in her pool. I'm acquainted with her mother. We sit and talk as the kids swim and splash in the pool. She asks me to read something she has written. I don't remember if it was a personal essay or a document for work, or why she even wanted me to read it. Upon leaving, script in hand, she kisses me on the lips. I'm flummoxed. I walk to my car feeling uneasy and somewhat violated. Why did she do that? Was she testing my friendship? Was it a form of aggression? Other friends kiss me goodbye, but on the cheek, or more accurately, the air beside my cheek.

*****

One day I'm in the basement doing laundry. I hear someone enter the house. It can't be the kids.

They're in school. Immediately, I think it's the black man from the PTA meeting who interrogated me with challenging questions the night before. I hear footsteps descending the stairs. *He is coming to kill me.* My heart races and I'm immobile. My son walks in the room. It takes me a moment to comprehend that it's David. His school let out early. I'm chagrined. Am I prejudiced after all or just a victim of the fear tactics created by the media?

I think about two other occasions when I thought I might be in harm's way, and both of them concern African-Americans and being frightened. I'm sitting alone in a large terminal waiting room when I spot a tall and peculiar looking black man in the distance. He fascinates me. I can't take my eyes off him. He starts walking in my direction. Then it becomes clear he is heading directly toward me, until he is just a few steps away. Then he swerves and walks on ahead. Perhaps he noticed me looking at him and wanted to scare me. He is successful. My heart is pounding.

*****

I'm in my forties—mid-life crisis time—and living in New Jersey. I feel unfulfilled. What do I do with the rest of my life? I seek counseling, and it takes weeks before I confess my dream of being an actress. The therapist encourages me to move forward with my desire. Months later, I work up the courage to register at HB Studio in Greenwich Village, Manhattan. I take a bus to New York in the morning to attend classes. One day I stay late to attend an audition at 6:00 p.m. at a location on 9th Avenue and 38th Street. Afterwards, I'm apprehensive about walking alone in the dark to the Port Authority. I ask if anyone is headed in that direction. The only offer I get is from a black actor. I accept, but wish he wasn't black. After all, I don't know him. But I don't know any of the white actors, either. When we get to the entrance, I thank him, believing he would go his way. But he says he'll stay with me until we reach the bus. We chat about acting. He is very nice and polite, yet I feel anxious and suspicious. Why does he want to walk me all the way to the bus? He stays with me until we reach the escalator going up to the platform. I thank him again for escorting me. I think he might have accompanied me up the escalator if I hadn't said it was all right for him to leave. I wonder if he felt my discomfort. Most likely he just wanted to be sure I was safe.

What has done this to me? Society, the media, the police? No, not the police. I'm white. I'm not stopped and frisked. I'm treated with some respect, albeit, as a woman, condescendingly rather than as a peer with a brain equal to a man's. I can feel it. It hurts. Yet I don't say anything. I don't know what to say. I accept my place in the social structure, and

quietly go on my way. How much more does an
African-American sense the humiliation?

*****

In 1987, my husband and I move to
Manhattan, and I attend classes led by Eric Morris.
His theory circles around the instrument (the actor)
and the craft (to fulfill the material). He assigns
exercises to release instrumental obstacles, such as
tension, fear, insecurities, and emotional blockages,
including sexual issues. He believes this frees his
students from *acting*, and allows their work to come
from a genuine place within when dealing with
emotions. His technique is quite controversial as it
can push the actor to raw and vulnerable depths.

An Upper East Side actress says, "I feel guilty
about my life of privilege. I was sent to the best
schools, I wear the best clothes. I never have to
worry about money. I see the world around me
suffer and struggle. I feel embarrassed and ashamed
that I should be this privileged while others are
discriminated against because of their poverty, race,
or religion."

It is the first time I hear the word "privilege"
associated with a similar life style as mine. I never
thought of myself as privileged, although my race
and affluence clearly makes me so.

207

I socialize with people whom I feel comfortable with because of shared interests, not because they belong to my socioeconomic group. Yet my youth was spent with families enjoying a similar environment as mine, so economic and racial differences were less noticeable. Now I'm living among a more diverse population. The privilege remark inspires me to look closer at the world, and acknowledge the bubble in which I've been living.

As I walk down the street, I try to imagine the life of passers-by. There is no shortage of individuals to choose from. I look at how people are dressed and groomed and if they walk tall and proud or slump, trying not to be seen. I watch riders on the subway, notice employees in stores and offices, and observe the population in different parts of town in order to understand the socioeconomic scale under which I live.

Sometimes I shadow a person and imitate their stride, an Eric Morris exercise called externals, which helps an actor create a character using your own physical body. It's amazing how altering my gait gives rise to a visceral sensation unlike my own natural one; I am literally walking in another's shoes. I follow a woman with a cane, a man who appears to be intoxicated, a well-dressed businessman, a shabby vagrant. Imitating another's physicality heightens my perception, but it does nothing to improve my own acting because I stay too much in my head.

The homeless are the easiest to recognize and the hardest to comprehend. I wonder how they live through the winter. I carry food bars with me and give them to the beggars who cross my path.

The acting years bring greater contact with minorities. By working with Asians, Latinos and African-Americans, these labels drop away and the words *acquaintance, scene partner, friend,* or even *enemy,* take their place.

In the fall of 2000, under the auspices of ARTGroup, I'm assigned to be assistant director for Elliott Williams, a black member of our company. He chose to direct a James Baldwin play called *Blues for Mr. Charlie.* I like Elliot, and we work together harmoniously.

A few weeks into rehearsal, he tells me he's moving to California and that I will have to take over the directing. I think he is being irresponsible. Why did he ask to do the play and accept the assignment of directing the play if he knew he might be moving? Why didn't he ask someone more experienced than I to be the assistant? I ask him why he can't wait until after the play is over to move. He tells me he was on the waiting list at a college with a top notch drama department, and had no idea beforehand that he would be accepted into the program. He says he just found out and classes are starting the following week.

I'm flustered. I'm angry. My heart is racing and my thoughts are scattered. *How can he do this to me? He's being unfair leaving me to direct a play I know nothing about. He chose the play because of the black theme, and now I'm stuck with it. What do I know about the subject? He has no right to walk out on this play.*

Eventually, I calm down, and realize that anyone would grab a chance to further a career if given an opportunity, and I can't blame Elliot for doing so. Did I blame Elliott's behavior on his race? Yes, I hate to admit it was probably my first response while in a panic. Is it possible that humans use race as an easy target, rather than believing your own kind would do such a thing? I like Elliot. He is intelligent, easy going and sociable, so why is that my first reaction when I lament the loss of his friendship?

I direct the actors the best I can, concentrating more on how they move around the stage rather than on the inner life of their characters. Anna, the Latino lead, and I are not working well together. She leaves in the middle of the run, and we have to find a replacement. The worst part is that

Anna left with my 1950's dress I loaned her for the role.

Anna is a different story. I'm angry that she walked out, only this time I don't mourn her absence, and I can never forgive her. However, I don't extend my dislike of Anna to her race.

Our group experiences many actors who quit during rehearsals, and one who doesn't show up opening night. Most of them are Caucasian. I now believe it had to do with the quality of our group, and that young actors were only trying to get ahead. Clearly, doing what is best for oneself has nothing to do with one's race.

I meet Maeve at the European Dissent/White Anti-Racist Group. I expect a discussion about ways to end discrimination, designations of volunteers for workshops, and demonstrations. Instead the group focuses on an individual's personal journey from prejudice to absolute tolerance. The meeting feels like group therapy. Everyone gets into a circle and says their name and pronoun they identify with, (she, he, they, Hir, Ze). We break into groups to talk about the subject of the evening which I believe had something to do with seeing yourself as an organizer. Maeve said, "We look within to find, and correct our own prejudice thoughts." I don't comprehend how this endeavor helps the greater cause against discrimination. I attend one more meeting without gaining clarity. Maeve and I meet and talk over lunch. I promise one more try at it, but life separates us for over a year when I contact her to get permission to use her name in this memoir. We have a long chat, and I agree to come to another meeting – sometime.

Eulogy: Leave 'em Laughing

My husband Stanley died sixteen days shy of our fortieth wedding anniversary. Our marriage was performed six weeks after we met and essentially acted as our sixth date. What drew us together so quickly? 'Twas our mutual sense of humor, topped by silliness, spontaneity, and puns.

Stanley was fond of asking an unsuspecting person, "Why did Josephine always cut up Napoleon's chicken for him?"

Answer: "Because she liked to take the bone apart."

All I could do was I stand there and cringe.

At the end of a delicious dinner at a fancy Manhattan restaurant, Stanley reached into his wallet and handed a credit card to the waiter, who promptly took it to get processed. He soon returned to the table, and humbly told Stanley that the restaurant could not take his card.

"Why not?" Stan asked.

"It's an Exxon card, Sir."

"Well, I got gas with my meal," Stan said.

He loved to joke with waiters, and if they laughed at his humor they were given an extra-large tip, but he never gave anyone less than 20%.

His ability to jest at any given situation prevented myriad arguments through the years. But as any spouse of a comedian can tell you, repeated gags became less and less funny as the marriage progressed. Yet fresh and clever jibes never failed to make me chuckle. He liked to play "Can You Top This" whenever I came up with a wisecrack, and he usually won the joust. The times when he didn't win (and I actually got *him* to laugh) felt like manna from heaven.

Several years before his death, Stanley was diagnosed with Mild Cognitive Impairment that gradually turned into Alzheimer's. He forgot words. He forgot numbers. He forgot names. Yet one thing remained constant, and unforgettable: his quick wit and humorous remarks.

When we went for an interview with the Administrators for Access-a-ride, a NYC Transit Agency that provides transportation for people with disabilities, Stan was apprehensive. He didn't want to go, yet once there, he was cheerful and co-operative. He answered all of the doctor's questions in an easy manner, although I knew he was feeling uncomfortable. When asked to spell the word

GHOST, he did it perfectly. "Can you spell it backward?" the doctor asked. "I certainly can," Stan replied. He arose from his chair, turned his back to the doctor, and spelled, G-H-O-S-T.

At his Celebration of Life ceremony, everyone who eulogized him commented on his sense of humor, and how it touched their funny bone. The next day I was overjoyed to learn from his caretaker, Candice, that Stan's last words were in the form of a pun. Candice would gently advise him of what nursing duty she was about to perform. "I'm going to take your blood pressure now," she would say, or "I'm taking the covers off so I can massage your legs."

Not long before he died, Candice was preparing to check Stanley's blood sugar. She lifted his hand, and stretched out his fingers to make the puncture, and said, "Now don't worry; it's just a little prick."

"Who told you?" he said.

Stan had always believed that his calling in life was to make people laugh. I hope he knows how successful he was at achieving that goal.

Made in the USA
Middletown, DE
09 August 2018